f**P**

the soul
of
psychotherapy

Recapturing the
Spiritual Dimension in
the Therapeutic Encounter

Carlton Cornett, L.C.S.W.

THE FREE PRESS

NEW YORK LONDON TORONTO SYDNEY SINGAPORE

THE FREE PRESS
A Division of Simon & Schuster, Inc.
1230 Avenue of the Americas
New York, NY 10020

Designed by Michael Mendelsohn of MM Design 2000, Inc.

Manufactured in the United States of America

10 9 8 7 6 5 4 3 2 1

Library of Congress Cataloging-in-Publication Data

Cornett, Carlton.
    The soul of psychotherapy: recapturing the spiritual dimension in the therapeutic
encounter/ Carlton Cornett.
        p. cm.
    Includes bibliographical references and index.
        1. Counseling.   2. Psychotherapy.   3. Spiritual life.
    4. Psychology and religion.   I. Title.
BF637.C6C586   1998
158'.3—dc21
                                                                                        97–32832
                                                                                            CIP

ISBN 0-684-83902-4

Dedicated with deep love, respect,
and enduring affection to:

ROSS HUDSON
חברי אחי
My Friend, My Brother

DeWAYNE FULTON
A Kind, Warm, and Gentle Spirit. My Soulmate

In memory of:
DAN WOOD
STUART BIVEN
Beloved Friends

Contents

Preface

I undertook writing this book with no small amount of trepidation. The potential pitfalls seemed numerous, and the path to producing something useful to clinicians seemed narrow indeed. One of the pitfalls is the fact that psychotherapy and spirituality have, at best, maintained a deeply ambivalent relationship with each other over the past century. Psychotherapists who speak of or write about spiritual issues are automatically suspect to more traditional clinicians, and with some justification. Increasingly, bookstore shelves are filling with so-called new age books, which claim a psychological basis but are short on rigorous clinical thinking.

On the other hand, spirituality has been the shadow cast on the consulting room wall from which we have tried to hide our eyes. There has been little systematic thought offered on addressing spiritual issues in psychotherapy. For a professional pursuit that prides itself on its uncompromising search for "the truth" of psychological functioning, psychotherapy has often gone to seemingly absurd lengths to avoid considering the possibility that the spiritual dimension deeply affects human life. The challenge became to write a book that calls attention to manifestations of the spiritual aspects of clients' lives and how to work with these in psychotherapy, but to do so in a way that is dynamically considered. In short, I have attempted to avoid this book's becoming like the old joke concerning the combination of a Jehovah's Witness and a Unitarian: knocking on doors for no apparent reason.

All books, indeed all interests, grow out of particular experiences. Psychotherapists' clinical interests generally grow out of the painful issues with which they have struggled. My interest in spirituality is no exception. For those outside my experience, it is important to know some of that struggle so that they can determine how generally applicable what I have to say may be.

I was reared in a family that was not particularly spiritually attuned. Like many other nominally Christian American families, we went to church—the United Methodist church—on Easter but on few other occasions. During my adolescence, which I remember as one of the bleakest periods in my life, I became more interested in the church. It offered an escape, even if only briefly, from what seemed incessant and devouring emotional turmoil and pain. The possibility that there might be a world beyond this one—a world that offered not only surcease of pain but even pleasure—was overwhelmingly attractive. After high school, I enrolled in a small United Methodist college and began to study history and psychology, with the ultimate goal of teaching. Early in my college experience, I received what I thought to be a call to the ministry through a dream and added the study of religion and philosophy to my majors. I now wanted to combine the ministry with psychological healing and hoped to become a pastoral counselor.

Through my studies, I encountered an array of spiritual and philosophical systems of thought, and as I did, I grew increasingly less convinced that Christianity had much to offer me or anyone else. Although it had probably literally saved my life as a younger adolescent, it grew to seem increasingly bereft of potential for a man not so near the emotional abyss. Further, it was at this period that I became increasingly aware, against my best efforts, of my homosexuality. I had struggled for years with this "affliction," and now it seemed inescapable. Being gay in the late seventies and early eighties presented some insurmountable problems for someone who wished to be a United Methodist minister. (Although slightly diminished, these obstacles remain today.) This capped the first of my great spiritual crises. Why would someone be blocked from serving God because of his or her sexual orientation? The question itself seemed to highlight my growing concerns about Christianity: is it a religion emphasizing love and tolerance, or one driven by prejudices cloaked in moral dogma? In my disappointment, I began to look more critically at the underpinnings of what I believed.

What I had not counted on was that searching my own beliefs regarding the very essence of life and death is more than an intellectual exercise. The adolescent who originally sought out God in desperation was back—with more questions, more dilemmas, and fewer certainties.

I settled on social work as a profession, because it allowed me to combine my interest in psychotherapy with an altruistic and ambitious hope that I could improve some segment of the world. Nevertheless, throughout my social work training and well into my early career, I struggled internally with what I believed about the spiritual nature of the universe. Christianity would not go away. It was a continual, albeit unwelcome, companion, along with the conviction that all that was eventually in store for me was hell. I entered psychotherapy with an older, very traditional psychoanalyst to address a number of depressive symptoms in my early twenties.

Like my adolescence, my first dynamically oriented psychotherapy is an experience I will probably always remember with a sense of bitter sadness and pain. My therapist, probably a well-meaning and certainly a learned clinician, stressed responsibility. There was nothing in life over which we have no control, he said. I grew over the relatively brief period I worked with him—about eight months—to perceive that he was starkly disappointed with me. The disappointment I perceived was not just his, though, but that of my father, and, although I probably could not have articulated it at the time, that of God as well. I was fired from a job after it was discovered that I was gay, even though I was more cautious about revealing that then. I came for a session a few days after the event hoping for some reassurance from him and instead met with a subtle rebuke that I had only myself to blame—always—for my difficulties in life. Although I ended my therapy with him at that time, I carried away from the experience the conviction that the universe found me a disappointment.

Over the following years, my spiritual and concomitant emotional struggles were never absent, though they were generally less intense. In my late twenties, I again sought out psychotherapy, again with a psychoanalyst, although one more interested in Heinz Kohut's psychology of the self. I have always been interested in self psychology, and we seemed a good fit. As I look back on my initial presentation to him, I blanch at how neurotically hopeless I must have seemed. I remember telling him that I wanted to be ready to die, although there was no indication that this would happen especially soon. He listened carefully to me, a hallmark of his style throughout our work together, and he was capable of hearing my spiritual struggles. Whereas my first analyst reduced all material to oedipal dynamics—competition, control—my second was willing to move into the realms of *my* psyche to understand the broader conflicts there: conflicts related to good and evil, the meaning of my life, values, and all the other foundational elements on which a spiritual understanding of life is constructed. I began this therapy with a picture of God as a being keeping lists, endless lists of offenses offered to him, and how he, with some glee, punished these offenses, primarily after the offender's death. This representation of God began to change during my second psychotherapy experience. This four-year period was one of the most important periods of my life. Ultimately I ended it with an entirely new perspective on God. Instead of a collector of wrongs, he might be more like a good parent—or a good therapist—a being who tried to understand why I do things rather than just condemn me. He might be capable of expressing a sense of pride in my accomplishments, sadness at my losses, and acceptance of my imperfect humanity.

Through both of these psychotherapy experiences, I began to understand the intimate relationship that exists between spirituality and psychotherapy. These experiences, as well as my clinical work, have convinced me that clients benefit when their distress is considered within a context that includes a spiritual dimension. Becoming a spiritually attuned psychotherapist is central to our lifelong training.

I seek to convey some of this relationship in the pages that follow. I do this with three caveats. First, my development was influenced by the Western Christian tradition. Further, most of my clients share a developmental foundation in this tradition. Therefore, throughout the book, concepts from this tradition will be utilized, even though the point may be to highlight the shortcomings of it. Like many of my clients, I have studied other spiritual traditions in a limited way and also present concepts from these traditions; however, the inescapable fact is that this book has a bias.

Anselm, one of the earliest Christian philosophers of religion, asserted that the fact that everyone (even a fool) knows to what he or she refers when speaking of God proves that God exists. Although this oversimplifies his argument, I believe it holds an important point. While it does not, in my estimation, prove the existence of God, it does suggest that a consciousness of monotheism is pervasive in Western culture. Similarly, when William James (1902) embraced religious experience and Freud (1927) rejected it, both argued from the inherent bias of the monotheistic tradition. Although their positions could not be more radically different, these opposing positions do not obviate the most basic bias. Whether one argues for or against something, one must begin with that something. In that lies what I believe is indeed a basic tenet of Western culture. Therefore, whether I like it or not (and I often do not), I approach this book with the basic monotheistic prejudice that is the legacy of development in a Western culture. For those who will criticize my discussion of spirituality and its manifestations in the therapeutic encounter as flawed because of this, I can only say that I agree and often wish ours was a more spiritually polymorphous culture.

A second caveat I would acknowledge at the outset is that this is a book primarily about spiritual distress. There is a good deal of lively and valuable discussion in the mental health literature regarding whether psychotherapists approach clients too much from a perspective of seeing their weaknesses versus their strengths. The psychodynamic tradition is particularly faulted in this regard. There is something of a double-bind in this for clinicians who write about their clinical work. On the one hand, the criticism that psychotherapy can be overly enamored of an individual's psychopathology versus healthy strengths is a valid one. However, clinicians see in their offices those in distress, not those for whom all is well. Therefore, in the vignettes throughout this book, there is more attention paid to the aspects of spirituality that arouse distress rather than those that are functional. Researchers and theorists who approach the issue of spirituality in a less turbulent, distress-laden environment will hopefully study the latter aspects of its presence in human life.

The final caveat I offer is that this book makes no attempt to present a new, systematic conceptualization of spirituality. The history of dynamic psychotherapy is a history of schism over theoretical descriptions.

Clinical theoreticians have often attempted to present a unique system of thinking about clinical phenomena. This has led to a confusing array of theories, often describing similar, if not identical, phenomena using different language. I have attempted to avoid overly theoretical discussions, and although I offer one definition of some of the elements of spirituality, I do not attempt a unified theory of the relationship between spirituality and psychotherapy. Instead, I want to propose that such a relationship exists and highlight some of the ways that it becomes manifest in the psychotherapeutic relationship.

Modern psychotherapists, like their predecessors the tribal shaman, are confronted with manifestations of spiritual yearning and conflict daily. However, unlike the shaman who embraced such manifestations and sought out their meanings, the psychotherapist has often turned away from them. As I write this, it has recently come to light that thirty-nine Heaven's Gate members killed themselves in such yearnings. Although such events are neither new, nor in this instance, even particularly staggering in relative scale, they are a grim and constant reminder that any endeavor seeking to understand the human dilemma cannot ignore the spiritual dimension.

Acknowledgments

The most enjoyable part of writing a book is thanking those without whose help it would not have come to fruition. For me, that is especially important because those people do not always know how invaluable a contribution they make unless I write it. Although they certainly know how much work goes into a book (because I constantly complain about it), I am not sure that they know how much I conceive it to be a team effort and how appreciative I am of their hard work. Now I have the opportunity to reflect that appreciation, however imperfectly.

First, my deepest appreciation goes to my partner, DeWayne Fulton. With each project, he endures my writer's block, reads endless drafts, tactfully but firmly points out three-page sentences, and, most important, always allows me to feel that he does so with pleasure. It is his great gift to be a man of grace, sincerity, and kindness, and at no other time is this gift more in evidence than when he helps me write.

Next, my appreciation goes to my colleague and friend of many years, Ross Hudson. Many of the ideas I write about have been bounced off him before they make it into print. He is unflagging in his willingness to tell me which ones are nonsensical and, although I may not always appreciate it at the moment it occurs, such interactions have been a great aid. Most important for this book has been his call at the end of the day to reassure me that it will be finished. It is always with pride that I call him my friend.

My editor at The Free Press, Philip Rappaport, deserves thanks. Not only did he suggest this book, but he encouraged me when I was not at all sure I could write it. Although I may have doubted my capability to write this book, I never doubted his editorial skill. He has done a good job of navigating this through the maze of publication. My thanks also to Beverly Brown, who typed portions of the manuscript with great skill.

Finally, my most sincere appreciation is due to my clients. I have led a richer life for having known each of them and learned innumerable lessons from their wisdom. To all of them, my thanks.

CHAPTER ONE

SPIRITUALITY

THE UNHEARD DIMENSION

It was a hot, humid, midsummer day outside my office. Inside I was sitting across from Mark, a man about my age who had been working with me in psychotherapy for about a year. He was talking about a sense of being stuck in his life. He had vocational and relational goals that he wanted to achieve and felt that he was making no progress toward these ends. Although I disagreed with his assessment that he had achieved nothing, I was aware that he found himself in cyclical patterns that maintained some unsatisfactory relationships in his life.

At one point during this particular hour, Mark mused about his frustration at being able to see these patterns but his seeming impotence to change them. Ultimately, he offered, in something more of a question than a statement, "I don't know whether it's my family and what I've learned from them that's holding me back, or that I'm supposed to learn something in this life that I'm not getting."

I quickly became aware of my reaction toward what Mark had just said. My very traditional psychodynamic training would suggest with certainty that it was the reenactment of old family dramas that kept Mark stuck. This training would have minimized, or ignored, the subtle undercurrent in his thinking that seemed spiritual in nature.

"What do you mean about learning something in this life that you're not getting?" I inquired.

"You know, the Eastern, maybe Buddhist, idea that we keep coming back until we learn the lessons that we're supposed to learn. That each life has an important lesson to teach us."

My mind returned to my training, which eschewed such mystical and esoteric thinking. I thought about my teachers and mentors who would surely refocus Mark on the role that internalized family dynamics—Representations of Interactions that have been Generalized (RIGs), in Stern's (1985) language—played in his unhappiness. However, Mark's spiritual question was not so easily dismissed for me.

"Perhaps it's both," I suggested. "I don't know that we have to see it as only one thing or the other. Life is generally much more complicated than that."

Mark looked at me with surprise, and a small grin nudged at the corners of his mouth. A veteran of therapy with a number of other clinicians, he explained that he had expected me to focus strictly on the familial dynamics of his dilemma. He asked if we could discuss areas related to spirituality.

"I'm not sure why we couldn't," I offered, "provided I'm not expected to have any of the answers." We both laughed.

Mark went on to talk about a number of spiritual conflicts in his life. Over the next several months, we explored his unsuccessful attempts to reconcile many aspects of his life with the religious upbringing of his childhood. Obviously some of this exploration involved the dynamics of his family. However, other aspects of it seemed to transcend this to the extent that he was attempting to create a new system of morals and ethics, new values, and a new sense of meaning in his life from the one his parents promulgated. He was, in essence, attempting to understand and create his spiritual system.

Later that same week, I was listening to another client, Bill, who also had been under the care of numerous other psychotherapists. On this particular day he revealed to me a deeply held belief that his agonizing depressive symptomatology was the result of God's condemnation of him for having taken the life of a small animal when he was a youngster. He argued that all would be changed if only he could be forgiven his childhood sadism. As I had with Mark, I listened with some internal conflict. I could have argued that this belief was the screen for a harsh and punitive superego and identification with one or both parents; it could also be argued that Bill's worries in this regard represented a form of "magical thinking" more appropriate to an earlier developmental epoch. But whatever the underlying dynamics, it was also a spiritual issue. Obviously Bill's harsh god was influenced by identifications with his parents. However, this was not the sum of it. He needed to talk about a system of morality and ethics that precluded forgiveness and instead was built on retribution for transgression and mistakes. We needed to discuss his god. His parents would play an important part in this discussion but would not be the entirety of it.

Parents can never be minimized in the creation of an individual's spiritual system. Nor can conflicts in the broader area of spirituality be reductionistically conceptualized as involving only identifications with parents. The Gestalt of an individual's spiritual belief system is constructed not only of familial influences but societal and cultural influences as well. Additionally, *spirituality is founded on reactions to what is fundamentally unexplainable by family and culture—phenomena such as the meaning of death, the mystery of the purpose of life, and the ultimate balance of the universe, which dictates the proportions of plausibly unexplainable fortune and setback in life.* It is, in short, the very essence of a view of the mysteries of life and, as such, a source of confusion, consternation, and conflict.

Mark and Bill exemplify some of this confusion and conflict. It has long been a cornerstone of psychotherapy that a clinician needs to explore whatever conflicts a client brings to the relationship. In the area of spirituality, however, the mental health disciplines have generally been resistant to dealing with spiritual issues overtly and frankly. M. Scott Peck asserted at a 1992 meeting of the American Psychiatric Association that American psychiatrists are poorly prepared to study or address spiritual phenomena due to cultural biases and that these biases have limited both the assistance that they can offer to clients and their own personal development (Lukoff, Lu, & Turner, 1995). This assertion was made in other mental health professions as well (Cornett,

1992b). Perhaps in response to such assertions the American Psychiatric Association's (1994) fourth edition of the *Diagnostic and Statistical Manual of Mental Disorders* lists a condition entitled "Religious or Spiritual Problem" that may be a focus of treatment. Despite this recognition, spirituality has been the unheard dimension in psychotherapy. Since spiritual issues form a major part of human life, it seems incredible that there would be resistance to the topic. Nevertheless, this resistance has a history almost as old as that of modern psychotherapy and a hold on current practice that is hard to loosen. Understanding this resistance requires looking at the history of psychotherapy and, most important, one of the philosophical or spiritual tenets on which that history is founded—what began as rationalism and has now become scientific positivism.

A BRIEF HISTORY OF PREMODERN PSYCHOTHERAPY: THE RISE OF RATIONALISM

Prior to discussing the relationship of spirituality to psychoanalysis, the earliest systematized method of psychotherapy, it is important to understand the social and cultural upheavals that shaped the nineteenth century and formed the context in which psychotherapy developed. For centuries psychological healing had been linked with spirituality and religion. The earliest psychotherapists were medicine men, priests and priestesses, prophets, soothsayers, and shamans (Bromberg, 1975; Ellenberger, 1970). These individuals were often viewed by their contemporaries as being divinely influenced or touched—hence the derivation of the term "to be touched." In early cultures and some current cultures less developed along Western lines, shamans have been sought out by troubled individuals because it was believed that they carried some special spiritual insight or enlightenment. Often these shamans began as deeply troubled people themselves, who spent years in internal struggle and turmoil. When this struggle ended and the person was seen to be at a greater level of peace, others in his culture assumed that he had seen the path to spiritual fulfillment illuminated by a divinity (Kopp, 1972). Interestingly, a similar process often occurs with modern psychotherapists, albeit without supernatural explanation. A troubled person begins the study of psychology to understand painful internal conflicts and ultimately decides to offer help to others through sharing what he or she has learned (Jamison, 1995). Jung (1963) commented on this phenomenon in his description of the "wounded healer." As a budding clinician pursues formal academic training, a more important experiential training takes place through this person's own psychotherapy or psychoanalysis. Generally therapists leave this experiential training somewhat more at peace than when it began. It is on this basis that our culture attributes authority to the psychotherapist. Like those who sought out a shaman, contemporary men and women, consciously or not, seek out a psychotherapist in the hope of learning something of the enlightenment that evolved from years of struggle with internal demons (Kopp, 1972). It is also to this phenomenon that we can attribute much of the disappointment that is currently attached to psychotherapy. It has not well withstood the weight of our projected wishes for spiritual contentment and the intentional or unintentional claims of its practitioners to be able to provide such contentment.

From the advent of Christianity to the Renaissance and Reformation periods, attempts to help those with psychological disturbances were generally the province of the Catholic church. The tools of this type of psychological aid were primarily moral exhortation, theological argument, and the confessional relationship (Ellenberger, 1970).

Probably the most important of these tools in terms of its real ability to provide psychological assistance was confession and the relationship that developed between a penitent and confessor. This private and insulated relationship allowed the penitent to unburden her or his soul in the complete assurance that it would remain confidential. It is no accident that confidentiality and privacy remain two cornerstones of modern verbal psychotherapy. Even after the Reformation, Protestant churches adopted a modified version of confession, *Seelsorge* ("cure of souls"), to address psychological and spiritual difficulties (Ellenberger,

1970). Hasidic Judaism also has an ancient practice focused on the relief of spiritual distress. The *yehidut* (private relationship) between the *rebbe* (master) and *hasid* (disciple) has many parallels to confession, *Seelsorge*, and modern psychotherapy (Schachter-Shalomi, 1991).

The difficulty inherent in the Catholic church's confessional system was that the relief it provided was to guilt and shame inflicted by its own dogma. The church, after all, defined those offenses requiring guilt, confession, contrition, and absolution. Often the foundations of moral prescriptions and proscriptions were not readily apparent or easily explained. Church authority provided the only absolute and final answer to a moral question, and generally there were a vast number of factors, including politics and economics, that informed such an authoritative answer. For centuries even the language in which religious tenets were formulated and communicated to the common people, Latin, was inaccessible to them. There was in this way an intractable ambivalence toward religion: it was simultaneously the arbiter of moral behavior, often inflicting guilt, based on ambiguous motivations presented in a confusing communicational medium, and a source of liberation from that guilt through the confessional relationship.

Perhaps more important to this discussion is the fact that on occasion official church doctrine was not congruent with the burgeoning evidence of the nature of the world. One example was the church's absolute maintenance that the earth was the center of the universe in response to Copernicus' challenge. Another was a similarly dogged conviction that the earth was flat rather than spherical. Holding views contrary to official church doctrine placed one in the greatest spiritual, and often physical, jeopardy. Laing (1967, 1969) describes similar processes in families as "mystification." A child who observes the evidence of one thing but is told not only that her perception is inaccurate but that the evidence supports an entirely opposite conclusion must choose which "reality" to trust. Such is the stuff that fosters schizophrenia. The reaction to the mystificational aspects of the church brought about just such a reaction.

With the Renaissance came the beginnings of a rejection of church doctrine in favor of a more rational, "objectively oriented" approach toward understanding the world and the universe. This rejection, initially tentative and subtle, grew steadily through the Enlightenment and reached full flower in the nineteenth century. This new rationalistic approach eschewed the value of that which was not observable or otherwise measurable as explanations for natural phenomena. It assumed a similar stance in regard to the psychological functions and motivations of the human being. In many cases, this approach did not even recognize the existence of phenomena like the soul that could not be observed or measured. This type of reasoning has not disappeared. Sagan (1996), for instance, offers a similar argument regarding the soul, citing an Enlightenment period experiment comparing the weight of a mouse's body just prior to death with the weight of that same body just after death. He interprets a lack of change in weight between the two states as evidence arguing against the existence of the soul, because the soul, like all other things, would be composed of matter and therefore have mass. The ancestral rationalism of Sagan's argument maintained that all aspects of the universe could ultimately be explained by natural laws. If a particular phenomenon could not be adduced from observable processes and events or by a known natural law, then it was assumed that this law existed and had simply not yet been discovered. Thus, this rationalistic philosophy became a system of spiritual thought because, reducing spirituality to its simplest element, it became a means of attempting to explain the unexplainable, the mysterious, in life. Rationalism had a number of eloquent spokesmen in the eighteenth and nineteenth centuries, including Voltaire and Rousseau in France, Thomas Jefferson and Benjamin Franklin in America, and Thomas Carlyle in England.

Late in the eighteenth century and into the nineteenth, this rationalistic philosophy combined with a period of rapid industrialization and urbanization. The industrialization of the West, which began during the Renaissance and reached its zenith in the middle and late nineteenth century, had a number of economic and cultural effects. It destroyed the feudal system and increased social mobility. Out of these economic changes grew social changes, including a more individualistic ethos, less anchored by and bound to family and cultural tradition and the previously enormously powerful influence of the church (Armstrong, 1993; Cushman, 1992, 1995). Cushman (1992) writes:

> Increased industrialization, urbanization, and secularization caused renewed interest in the physical world, the humanities, science, commerce, and rationality. However, the evolving self, ever more individual, presented new problems for the emerging modern state. The state had to develop ways to control a new kind of subject: more mobile, less constrained by tradition and religion, less confined by role, and less predictable. (p. 25)

In addition to the increased mobility and individualization that distanced people from familial and religious traditions, industrialization brought with it an increased interest in material goods as more was available to the common person. Thus, consumerism became a potent motivation in the broader societal psyche. This, Fromm (1950) argues, also posed a dramatic challenge to traditional, especially religious, tenets and institutions:

> People go to churches and listen to sermons in which the principles of love and charity are preached, and the very same people would consider themselves fools or worse if they hesitated to sell a commodity which they knew a customer could not afford. Children in Sunday school learn that honesty and integrity and concern for the soul should be the guiding principles of life, while "life" teaches us that to follow these principles makes us at best unrealistic dreamers. (p. 2)

In Laing's language, the mystification of the church had been replaced by a secular mystification based on rationalism and its resultant social developments. At best, the result was profound confusion (Silverstein, 1993). Fromm (1950) describes it at its worst as "spiritual chaos and bewilderment dangerously close to a state of madness . . . a madness akin to schizophrenia in which the contact with inner reality is lost and thought is split from affect" (pp. 1–2). It was at the height of both the ascendancy of rationalism and its resultant social upheavals that Sigmund Freud emerged with his psychoanalytic technique.

RATIONALISM AND SPIRITUALITY IN PSYCHOANALYSIS

Freud, who can be fairly credited with the advent of modern psychotherapy, seems to have been deeply ambivalent about the role of spirituality in psychoanalysis. His writings support various interpretations of the place of spirituality in human life. The majority of Freudian apologists maintain that Freud, like any other scientist, had little use for such a "soft" concept as spirituality, and there is evidence in his writings to support such a position. However, two important psychoanalytic voices have argued the other side of Freud's ambivalence. For instance, both Bettelheim (1982) and Fromm (1950) point out that he named his fledgling method *psycho*analysis, founded, like the terms *psychology* and *psychiatry*, on the Greek word *psyche*, or "soul." Bettelheim (1982) also points out that one of the words, *seele*, now represented in Freud's writing as *ego*, is actually more faithfully translated into English as *soul*. Bettelheim contends that Freud viewed the soul, not a mechanistic ego, as the seat of human identity and uniqueness. He has argued that Freud was keenly aware of the spiritual dimensions of his work and that this awareness was diluted and suppressed primarily by translators and disciples eager to develop a more widely acceptable and respected profession. Fromm too maintains that much of what supports a rejection of spirituality in Freud's writing stems from early in his career. The mature Freud, he contends, viewed human motivations much more broadly and inclusively. Fromm further argues that Freud had a deep respect for the spiritual realm, as evidenced by his immersion in the gods and goddesses of antiquity. The arguments of both Bettelheim and Fromm illuminate an important aspect of Freud's views of spirituality. The evidence, however, suggests that he was concerned about the acceptance of his method by the larger public. He was also anchored in the rationalist tradition, which hampered consideration of anything that could be known only through intuition rather than objective, scientific observation and reasoning.

Freud was devoted to nineteenth-century rationalism. As Gay (1988) points out, Freud was influenced by the idea that reason could set right the ills of the world through its application in science and the scientific method. He also viewed science and spiritual systems such as religion as irreconcilable opposites, as did many of his early adherents. Ernest Jones offered a summation of the psychoanalytic view of religion in a 1911 letter to Freud in which he asserted that religion was "the last and firmest stronghold of what may be called the anti-scientific, anti-rational, and anti-objective *Weltanschauung*" (Gay, 1988, pp. 533–534).

Although Freud surely understood the differentiation of religion from the broader concept of spirituality, religion being only one form of spiritual expression, he seemed keenly aware that the majority of people in the Western world did not. The Judeo-Christian monotheistic tradition, which continues to dominate Western spiritual thought, actively discourages considering spirituality apart from religion. Through loose interpretations of proscriptions such as the first of the Ten Commandments ("You shall have no other gods before Me"), the monotheistic traditions have sought to equate religion with spirituality. The result has been a generalized confusion of these disparate phenomena.

The confusion of spirituality and religion remains (Coles, 1995). Additionally, Freud was quite critical of the role organized religion played in culture. He described it as an "illusion" serving to aid in the denial of mortality (1927) and saw it as a means of social control (1913, 1939). Thus, organized religion and its expression were generally proposed to serve primarily neurotic ends. Perhaps more important, however, Freud's often accurate criticisms of the intrapsychic and social functions served by organized religion seem to have become the standard lens through which all spiritual expression is viewed. Psychoanalysts have traditionally conveyed open disdain for all religious expression, because to do otherwise would suggest neurosis in the analyst. Even Thomas Szasz, the iconoclast who has challenged psychiatry and psychoanalysis on so many important issues, follows the traditional line on religion: "Religion is the denial of the human foundations of meaning and of the finitude of life; this authenticated denial lets those who yearn for a theo-mythological foundation of meaning and who reject the reality of death to theologize life" (1994, p. 35). This view is still generally consistent in the contemporary analytic culture and is captured by Fine (1979) in his bold statement that "no prominent analyst today could be said to believe that religion has any real value for mankind" (p. 449).

Although many of Freud's insights about organized religion were accurate, the analytic movement's concerted attempts to separate itself completely from all religious expression led to a stifling of thought about the much broader spectrum of spiritual expression. It is also worth noting that psychoanalysis, which, as a collective profession, was so adamantly against organized religion, created its own religion, complete with a priesthood and dogma of salvation, which included the rejection of all other religions (Masson, 1990).

There seems to have been another, more subtle factor in Freud's determination that psychoanalysis not be associated with religion in any way. Freud seems to have internalized the antisemitism of his time and wanted above all else to avoid the world seeing psychoanalysis as "Jewish," which he was convinced would marginalize it (Gay, 1988). He embraced C. G. Jung, the son of a Protestant minister and by far the most mystical of his early disciples, because adding Jung to his coterie would lend it credibility. In letters to Karl Abraham, who was angered by Jung's provocative theoretical challenges, Freud counseled patience, asserting that "only his [Jung's] appearance has saved psychoanalysis from the danger of becoming a Jewish national concern" (Gay, 1988, p. 204). So in addition to his rejection of religion because of its "antiscientific" characteristics, religion and spirituality had to be neglected as legitimate areas of study for the psychotherapist because of the political and economic consequences that would accrue to not doing so.

Although antisemitism has decreased as a motivating force, the objections to including spirituality in a comprehensive personology remain in contemporary psychoanalytic thinking. Succeeding generations of psychoanalysts, as well as psychotherapists of other theoretical orientations, have pursued the mantle of scientific credibility for psychotherapy for a variety of reasons. Psychotherapists have sought to compare the healing that occurs in their offices with that of physicians and medical science. Often this has had economic motivations. Western society, the cradle of psychotherapy as we now conceive of it, bestows financial acceptance—from grants to fees—on those activities that conform to rationalistic, often labeled "scientific," tenets. For psychology, chief among these tenets is the notion that human behavior is explainable, predictable, and ultimately controllable with accurate knowledge and the application of that knowledge.

The rationalism that shaped Freud has not disappeared, though it is now generally referred to as scientific positivism. It has lost much of its innocence in two world wars and the irrational and murderous upheavals of the twentieth century, but it is still very much the dominant force in Western thought. Sagan (1996), concerned that this view not lose its dominance, warns that the devaluation or rejection of scientific, objective thinking endangers both the foundations of Western civilization and democratic principles.

As a philosophy, rationalism or positivism deserves respect—but no more than any other. It must not be the spiritual system that crushes all others in psychotherapy.

JUNG AND THE POST-JUNGIANS

There is an important note of dissension regarding the need to ignore spirituality within the psychodynamic tradition. This note has been sounded by Jung and his followers who demonstrate through their work a decided fascination with the spiritual aspects of life. The theoretical break between Freud and Jung was at least partially the result of Jung's inclusion of spiritual concerns in his model, resulting in a diminution of weight afforded to sexuality as the prime human motivator (Fromm, 1950).

Jung shared Freud's ambivalent attachment to rationalism. Jung reported that he discovered the anima, the feminine component of the personality, when he asked himself during self-analysis if his work was "science," and the answer came back that his work was not science but instead "art." Ultimately he rejected this answer and decided that the anima could be deceptive (Ellenberger, 1970). His reflection, however, offers some evidence that Jung's unconscious was open to viewing the world through a nonpositivistic lens.

Post-Jungians seem to be much less ambivalent about viewing the world nonpositivistically. It is to such post-Jungians as James Hillman (1996) and Thomas Moore (1992) that a popular revival of interest in spirituality and healing owes much. Jungians such as Elkins (1995) have consistently argued that spirituality—the soul—cannot be removed from the psychotherapy office. Also important to note is that Jungians have been open to integrating their psychological insights with Eastern religious and spiritual systems (Kawai, 1996; Spiegelman & Miyuki, 1985). Academic psychology has consistently pursued a positivistic course, first through its love affair with behaviorism and currently in its infatuation with physiology and perception. Psychiatry has simultaneously turned to biological explanations for psychological life. The Jungians and post-Jungians have offered a perpetual challenge to this reductionistic trend. This challenge has also been offered in a disciplined way that separates a respectful, open curiosity from the opportunism of much of the so-called new age movement.

Where the Jungian tradition has not fulfilled its potential has been in its subtle deemphasis of the individual in pursuit of collective or archetypal answers. This again seems to be an attempt to reduce or eliminate the mystery of life. This pursuit suggests that all is ultimately explainable, yet that is not the human condition.

A POSTMODERN CONSTRUCTIONIST PERSPECTIVE

Hillman and Ventura (1992) propose that "we've had a hundred years of analysis and . . . the world is getting worse and worse" (p. 3). They argue that psychotherapy has not been of optimal benefit to humanity because it has focused us away from the external world and extinguished the motivations for changing that world through economic and political means. It has instead turned all our attention toward the internal world. Although I do not agree with all their reasoning, I believe their basic premise to be sound. Certainly countless individuals have been aided, but the world collectively has not necessarily been improved by psychotherapy. The reasons for this are obviously complex and diverse, but one reason often overlooked is that psychotherapy has been much too focused on the control of society through the adaptation of the individual. It has become the tool that the modern state needed to control its increasingly individualistic subjects (Cushman, 1992, 1995; Szasz, 1994). In the area of spirituality, psychotherapy has redirected our attention away from the unavoidable angst of the ambiguity of our lives and the intensely personal search for spiritual fulfillment. It has, instead, albeit subtly and generally without conscious awareness by its practitioners, promulgated one philosophical-spiritual worldview: positivism.

The twentieth century, however, has seen a response to the rationalistic-positivistic tradition, initially through the symbolic interactionism articulated by Margaret Mead, then through existentialism, and most recently through constructionism, which has its roots in both traditions. Constructionism challenges the fundamental notion of positivism that science (or, for that matter, any other system of thought) can ultimately explain the universe through the identification and elaboration of natural laws. It relies on the subjective construction of meaning rather than assuming an objective a priori meaning of phenomena. It is what the subject, influenced by the cultural environment, makes of the event that is crucial in giving it meaning, not the event itself (Burr, 1995).

Social constructionism has generally been concerned with language and a culture's ability to shape reality through its language. For instance, Burr (1995), like Orwell (1949) in 1984, argues that if there is no word for a particular concept in a culture, then there is no identification of the concept or phenomenon itself. Hence, something exists or fails to exist based on whether it can be articulated through a culture's language.

Social constructionism has actually always had a foothold in psychotherapy, beginning with Freud's interest in emotions. It is generally a given in modern psychotherapy that emotions are important. However, this was one of the truly innovative and novel aspects of psychoanalysis (Fromm, 1950). Freud introduced the idea that emotions influence the assignment of meaning to a phenomenon, and vice versa. This was a radical challenge to the rationalist tradition. Another was his subordination of the seduction theory, which postulated that an actual objective trauma fostered neurosis, to the theory of oedipal development. In the latter theory, he proposed that the oedipal developmental epoch was both universal and deeply influenced by fantasy and that it was the meaning ascribed to this period, elaborated in fantasy, that determined its impact on life. However, this constructionist trend was contained within a positivist framework (the natural law of psychosexual development).

Constructionism began to achieve a consistent influence on psychotherapy with the development of four clinical models: two within the psychoanalytic tradition and two as outgrowths of it. These four models—the interpersonal approach, the client- or person-centered approach, existential theory, and self psychology—placed subjectivity in a superordinate position.

Interpersonal theory, the oldest of these models, had its origins in the work of Sandor Ferenczi, one of Freud's earliest disciples, who, like many other psychoanalytic rebels, broke with him over the latter's rigid conviction that all clinical situations must be approached with the same mind-set and manner. Freud's ambivalent attachment to rationalism again surfaces in this area; although he demanded that psychoanalysts follow a strict, almost antiseptic clinical methodology, he was far from his own orthodoxy in working with clients (Gay, 1988; Thompson, 1994). It seems Freud knew that psychotherapy is not a universally applicable method but an idiosyncratic experience; however, he could not free himself of his deeply ingrained rationalist worldview to commit this to his writings. The interpersonalists, however, did address this theme in a focus on the therapeutic experience.

Interpersonal theory was most persuasively argued in the West, especially the United States, by Harry Stack Sullivan (1953b). Sullivan proposed that the therapist can never be an objective arbiter or interpreter of the client's experience. Instead, the therapist is inseparably entwined in the clinical encounter and her or his subjective responses to the client, and the unfolding relationship between them invariably influences that relationship and the process of therapy. The interpersonal tradition therefore views psychotherapy as a reciprocally influenced endeavor that must take into account the subjective experiences of all participants (Levenson, 1995).

The second model began with the work of Carl Rogers (1951) at the University of Chicago in the 1950s. The client-centered, now referred to as person-centered, approach offers two radical challenges to standard psychotherapeutic dogma: that people have within them an innate tendency toward psychological growth or self-actualization and that, by focusing on the client's subjective experience through empathic immersion in her or his world, this innate tendency can be activated. Interestingly, although Rogers and his colleagues focused on the subjective clinically, there has always been a strong research component to this approach. While psychoanalysts maintained that their approach was scientific in nature, they resisted attempts at research. Rogers asserted that psychotherapy had traditionally been "an art which made a pretense of being a science" (Kirschenbaum, 1979, p. 205). Conversely, Rogers and his colleagues cultivated research on their theory and have produced some of the most sophisticated research on psychotherapy to date (Zimring & Raskin, 1992).

The third model, the existential, evolved in the intellectual tradition of Otto Rank (1964) and was first systematically articulated by Jean-Paul Sartre (1956). Existential psychotherapy focuses on the individual's subjective creation of meaning in a morally ambiguous world. Existential psychotherapy has been most overtly concerned with spirituality, assuming it to be a source of both anxiety and comfort. Sartre's work focuses on the role that spiritual needs play in life. His conviction regarding the centrality of spirituality in life is captured in his statement that "to be man means to reach toward being God. Or if you prefer, man fundamentally is the desire to be God" (p. 566). Similarly, he argues for the constructionist view of spirituality: "in a word, God, if he exists, is contingent" (p. 81). Existential psychotherapy's most articulate contemporary proponent, Yalom (1980), focuses on spirituality through the individual's confrontation with death and the necessity of creating meaning in a finite life.

The final model, self psychology, originated in the work of Heinz Kohut (1977, 1984). Self psychology focuses on the developmental progression of narcissism and the attainment of a cohesive, coherent identity. Key to this development is hypothesized to be the experience of being responded to empathically. Self psychologically oriented psychotherapists focus on creating an environment of empathic understanding. Also important in regard to spirituality, self psychology postulates that human beings have an innate need to transcend themselves through merging with something larger than themselves. The idealizing selfobject need, discussed in more detail in Chapter 4, offers a developmental perspective on the crucial role that spirituality plays in life. Interestingly, self psychologists have afforded scant attention to this dimension of their theory, probably because for most of its formative years, self psychology struggled to be accepted as a part of traditional psychoanalysis and avoided controversy in as many areas as possible. Self psychology shares much with interpersonal theory, existentialism, and person-centered psychology (Atwood, 1989; Bromberg, 1989; Cornett, 1992a; Kahn, 1989).

This book builds on these traditions and focuses on offering an alternative to the positivistic approach to psychotherapy. Each of these traditions offers an alternative approach, from a constructionist foundation, which allows a phenomenological perspective on spirituality. Each client will be seen as developing a unique spiritual worldview out of an idiosyncratic set of circumstances and dynamics. A constructionistic approach does not assume an objective, externally definable reality, but holds instead that reality is inherently subjective. Put more simply, reality is relative. It is relative to a number of factors: the history and culture of the person experiencing a given phenomenon, the person's perceptual acuity or anomalies, and most important, her or his expectations. Most of what is referred to as Reality is a consensual expectation by a given group of people that a certain object or phenomenon has a mutually understood set of qualities or properties. One has only to hear two people discuss an event that they both experienced to understand how relative reality truly is. Reality is especially relative to cultural expectations. Those phenomena that we in the industrialized Western world might consider miraculous might be considered commonplace in a more "primitive" culture, and vice versa.

A constructionist approach to psychotherapy has roots in the Platonic tradition. It acknowledges the possibility that what is perceived as reality may be only a perception of the shadow of a phenomenon or an incomplete rendition of it. In a poem originally published in 1827, Edgar Allan Poe captures the possibility always before constructionism:

> All that we see or seem
> is but a dream within a dream. (1827/1938, p. 967)

In fairness it must be acknowledged that this, like rationalism and modern positivism, is a spiritual stance. It attempts to account for the mysterious and unexplainable in life by asserting that these are created subjectively by the individual, who must assume ultimate responsibility for resolving them. In this way it locates the answer to life's mysteries as internal rather than external. As a spiritual stance, it is as suspect as positivism when applied to psychotherapy. However, constructionism has an important built-in safeguard in its refusal to concede superiority to so-called objective (consensually defined and enforced) reality over subjective reality. In this way such an approach prevents the psychotherapist from becoming an arbiter, and ultimately enforcer, of cultural prejudices and expectations masquerading as fact or reality (Fromm, 1980; Szasz, 1994). Especially in regard to spirituality, it is crucial that psychotherapy allow the client to define a reality that can be comfortably lived.

Another potential strength and weakness of a constructionist approach to psychotherapy is in the areas of causation and linearity. Constructionistic thought eschews linear thought in causation, a challenge and an opportunity to psychotherapy. Most of us practicing psychotherapy have theories regarding the causal factor(s) of psychological difficulties. Generally these etiological theories are composed of linear reasoning: A leads to B. A constructionistic approach, because it questions the nature of A and B, questions as well the utility of supposing that one influences, much less causes, the other. It is impossible to avoid causal thinking completely in psychotherapy, nor would it necessarily be useful to do so. The result would be a chaotic quagmire. However, the opportunity it offers to psychotherapy is to encourage a bit more chaos, especially regarding spirituality, than we often tolerate. It discourages the hubris that seductively insinuates that we can explain everything. Most simply put, it returns the humanity to an encounter between human beings.

The chapters that follow explore a number of factors, both familial and cultural, as potentially formative in the development of a spiritual worldview. Chapter 2 reviews some of the factors that comprise a spiritual perspective or cosmology. Through this review, an operational definition of spirituality is offered.

Chapters 3 and 4 explore the development of spirituality. Chapter 3 highlights the role that parental identifications play in this development, and Chapter 4 places spiritual development in the context of narcissistic development.

Chapters 5 and 6 focus on one of the most difficult dilemmas of human existence: the emotional and spiritual integration of love and hatred. Chapter 5 places both love and hatred in a developmental context and argues for viewing both as legitimate, indeed indispensable, aspects of emotional and spiritual life. Chapter 6 explores the tendency to seek a form of tenuous security by clinging to various forms of moral absolutism, even at the expense of emotional and spiritual authenticity.

Chapters 7 and 8 concern spiritually attuned clinical technique. Chapter 7 explores the psychotherapist's contributions to the encounter with a client and some of the more prominent potential difficulties that may reside in the therapist's spiritual values and perspective. Chapter 8 explores the atmosphere created by the spiritually attuned clinician that facilitates the resolution of spiritual pain and encourages spiritual growth.

Finally, a reflection is offered on the importance of clients' integrating an affirming spiritual perspective into their lives. This integration, one of the most important tasks of life, is ideally suited to the psychotherapeutic endeavor.

The primary goal of this book is to offer a perspective for psychotherapists willing to hear the spiritual dimension in clinical work with clients. Such a perspective challenges therapists to explore their own cherished spiritual beliefs, and thus offers opportunities for both anxiety and growth. The key tenet of this perspective is that there is no universal, uniform pattern to which spirituality adheres. Indeed, the complexity of human life defies even the most elegant and seemingly comprehensive of theories. Jung (1963) captured this quality when he acknowledged that the psychotherapeutic process had been different with every client. Kopp (1972) similarly likens every psychotherapeutic endeavor to a journey with no identifiable destination at the outset.

I hope this book captures some of the flavor and elements of this journey. As I often tell clients as we begin therapy, there may be no answers here. Our best hope is to illuminate some of the questions more clearly. In the pages that follow, I seek to illuminate some of the questions involved in the process of a psychotherapy that seeks to understand and aid clients with the spiritual dimensions of their lives. The first question involves looking at what might comprise spirituality.

CHAPTER TWO

DEFINING SPIRITUALITY

Our wish [is] to persuade ourselves that we have once and for all fathomed the mysteries of the universe, our desire to make our mark during that moment of eternity in which we appear and disappear.

—ROBERT COLES, *THE MIND'S FATE*

One of the traditional difficulties associated with considering spirituality within the context of psychotherapy has been the inherent difficulty in defining it. Spirituality is such a broad and nebulous concept that it seems to have often intimidated those who would place it in a context for discussion. This, along with the general sense of confusion that equates spirituality with religion, creates unease for many psychotherapists and has kept spirituality on the periphery of clinical thinking. This chapter presents a clinically accessible operational model of spirituality in which I highlight six of the most clinically relevant elements of spirituality: meaning in life, values, mortality, organization of the universe, suffering, and transcendence.

MEANING IN LIFE

One of the frequent complaints that contemporary clients bring to psychotherapists is that life lacks meaning. The Rankian analyst Esther Menaker (1989) observes that "the present-day population suffers

21

primarily from a sense of alienation, from a loss of meaningfulness in life, from disillusionment and an absence of faith in themselves and others" (pp. 75–76). This alienation and disillusionment take various forms, from the direct assertion that life is meaningless to the more subtle symptoms of an empty depression comprising a lack of motivation and initiative. One example of a client with such a depression was Ed.

Ed was a middle-aged man who came for therapy because of a constant low-level, nagging depression. He felt generally dysphoric, and little in life aroused his excitement or, for that matter, his attention. Initially he focused almost exclusively on the symptoms of his depression. Our sessions were full of discussions of his difficulty in concentrating, lack of sleep, and general irritability. Whenever I attempted to look beyond symptomatology for the dynamics that might underlie these symptoms, he quickly returned me to looking at the manifest content of his depression. After a couple of months of feeling somewhat stuck with Ed, I referred him to a psychiatrist for a chemotherapy evaluation. Ed was placed on an antidepressant, and his symptoms began to improve.

During sessions subsequent to his being placed on the antidepressant, he became almost completely silent. Initially I had conceptualized his almost obsessive focus on his symptoms prior to being placed on medication as resistance. After he started the medication, I interpreted his silence from this same perspective. However, it became clearer and clearer to me that this was not an accurate assessment. Gradually it became apparent that his initial focus on his symptoms reflected his attempt to communicate about the only thing that really meant anything to him. His symptoms were real to him as nothing else was. Beyond this, his life lacked any central meaning. The depression, with its tangible symptoms, at least provided some meaning for his life. When these symptoms were partially alleviated by the antidepressant, he lost the minimum of comfort that they provided.

When I could finally move past the idea of seeing his focus on symptoms and his silence as resistance, I proposed to him the possibility that he had nothing to talk about because nothing seemed real or meaningful. He broke into tears, and we finally began to slowly explore the meaninglessness of his life.

Ed's depression is not an uncommon syndrome or an especially new one. Forty years ago May (1953) observed such depressive states, characterized by a sense of emptiness and meaninglessness, in his clients with such regularity that he labeled the twentieth century the Age of Emptiness. Over the intervening decades since May proposed this radical conceptualization, it seems to have become ever more descriptive of the motivations that impel clients to seek out psychotherapists. Indeed, it seems to be one of the most common difficulties for which people consult a psychotherapist.

When clients experiencing such a depression talk about it, they are often focused on the manifest expression of that depression. If pressed, more insightful clients acknowledge a sense of emptiness that goes along with the traditionally conceived depressive symptoms. This type of empty depression reflects a deeply felt deficit in the ability to attach meaning to one's life. Faced with such an existential dilemma, it is not at all surprising that one would feel despair and hopelessness, the hallmarks of today's depression.

Interestingly, one of the dilemmas for modern mental health practice is a controversy regarding antidepressants. There are those, especially biologically oriented psychiatrists, who argue that depression, as well as most other mental health difficulties, is the result of brain chemistry and function. Opponents to this view, primarily psychodynamically oriented therapists, argue that medications mask the true dynamics of a client's difficulties and therefore are a hindrance to treatment. There is a growing consensus of middle-ground belief that medications can be helpful because there are some brain functions and brain chemistry involved in many forms of psychopathology. On a much deeper level, however, the issue of using medication versus not using medication misses the point. Medications can certainly be helpful in aiding clients to manage the troubling symptoms of depression. They can make life generally more livable and less a source of interminable despair. One of the other useful functions that medications, especially antidepressants, can serve is that they highlight what is missing once the symptoms are taken away. In many cases, the absence of meaning in life is what is highlighted once depressive symptomatology is controlled.

Hillman (1996) argues that the central task of each person is to find *a* meaning in his or her life. He highlights the confusion that often attends the distinction between *a* meaning and *the* meaning of life. Clients often seem to believe that there is one overarching meaning that should be attached to all people's lives. In other words, we are all on this world for the same central reason, with the same tasks and dilemmas. Over the years of my practice, I have discovered that an important component of a client's depression is often the conviction that he or she has missed out on what everyone else knows. Others, they believe, know *the* answer. This belief can lead to the sense of utter alienation that feeds despair.

The task for the psychotherapist is to aid each client in challenging this conceptualization and then discovering and creating *a* meaning for life. Consistent with the constructionist's view, it would be unhelpful to assume that there is one universally applicable meaning that can be discovered through the process of psychotherapy. Instead, the therapist aids the client in both discovering values that provide a central focus of life and constructing a meaning based on those values.

VALUES

Psychotherapy has always been concerned with values. The earliest attempts to conduct psychotherapy were generally related to specific cultural or religious values. For instance, the confessional relationship had a specific set of values as its bedrock. These values were developed by the Catholic church and disseminated to (or imposed on, depending on your vantage point) its adherents. These values were thus originally externally created for most people (influential theologians being somewhat an exception).

The advent of psychoanalysis brought a radically new vision of values. Freud's earliest interests included the role of values in human functioning, although he discussed them as a rationalist. Freud's earliest work, now sometimes labeled id psychology, was concerned with those instinctual impulses that press for expression in a variety of disguised ways. He began with the proposition that human beings are born with innate needs, which they often strive to repress in various ways to meet cultural expectations but which nevertheless find symbolic expression. Put in more modern terminology, he proposed that the human being is constitutionally hardwired to some extent. The truly radical aspect of his thought was that what was denied open expression and why was crucial. This went to the heart of exploring values. Coles (1970) captures this well in his description of Freud's primary goal as understanding "from a new vantage point *some* of the reasons people have the beliefs they do, treat children the way they do, work at what they do, eat as they do, or love when and in the manner they do" (p. 57).

It is often argued that much of Freud's early professional rejection was the result of his assertion that sexuality, especially infantile sexuality, plays an important part in human development. However, it could also be argued that the chilly reception afforded Freud by his colleagues when his work was first presented was due to the fact that he suggested that values were, to a large extent, the creation of the individual and this questioned the idea that values were externally created and imposed. Paradoxically, in this challenge Freud offered the potential for both great comfort and equally great suffering. The view was now offered of the individual self as master, within constitutional constraints, of life's trajectory. In this lay the comfort of being able to exceed the bounds of culturally imposed values. But in this also lay the suffering. What Freud pointed out was that we create many of our own values, always in commerce with the larger culture, including our families. As this notion has permeated Western culture, it has had a profound influence because, to a great extent, it struck down the safety of externally imposed values. The void created by this decrease in externally imposed values has to be filled, a devastatingly difficult task for many people. In an insightful exploration of the seemingly growing prevalence of borderline personality states, Silverstein (1993) states:

> But if the individual has been freed from outmoded social and sexual roles, he is nonetheless forced to exact a price for his freedom—to make choices—and this freedom invariably results in personal confusion and conflict. . . . [Borderline personality disorder] is a direct result of these changing social norms in the twentieth century, . . . it is, in a sense, a social dilemma created by freedom. (p. 125)

Intimately tied to establishing meaning in life is the organization of values into a coherent system that supports a viable view of the self. One of the difficulties that clients often bring to the psychotherapist is a system, whether consciously articulated or not, of values that do not support such a view. Rather, the system in place when clients begin therapy is often contradictory to fundamental aspects of themselves. Put simply, many clients strive to be something that is not authentic to their temperaments or histories.

Broadly defined, values refer to those principles by which an individual makes decisions regarding the conduct and trajectory of life. In a very narrow sense, this can refer to ethical parameters. However, for purposes of this discussion, values are considered in a broader context as referring to those things that an individual values in life.

As a consequence of the attempt to adhere to a system of values that is not resonant with their basic temperaments and histories, clients often present with conflicts regarding a sense of priority in their lives. They literally seek to discover what is important to them. Again, as much as discovering what is important, the process of therapy helps them to construct and establish what is important to them. One example of a client struggling with issues related to values was Sarah.

Sarah originally presented for therapy in her mid-twenties to explore anxieties related to social events, especially speaking events, an important part of her work. She talked about panic attacks prior to any major presentation or other social activity on which much of her work depended.

Early in therapy, Sarah's anxiety regarding public speaking seemed to represent difficulties with the modulation of self-esteem and comfort with assertiveness, but it soon became apparent that this was not the entire story. As therapy progressed, Sarah's deeply conflicted view of the value that she placed on her work came to the fore. Both parents had lived during the Great Depression, and both held a sincere and devout belief that security, especially financial security, is to be prized above all else. Sarah had attempted to incorporate this value from her parents, but her well-paid work was not especially satisfying to her.

Over the course of her therapy, Sarah and I looked at the values that seemed most to be guiding her life's trajectory. One of the outcomes of her therapy was a realignment of those values, which included satisfaction with her work. Ultimately Sarah left her job and started her own business, one that was much more in keeping with the ways she wanted to spend her days. Although her parents were quite startled and against this move, Sarah recognized that it would be important for her to experience her work with some joy as well as seeing it as a source of financial security.

Sarah's case is not at all unusual in our particular culture. As Fromm (1950) and Cushman (1995) point out, consumerism and money have long been important cultural values. Probably the two most common crises that impel clients to seek the services of a psychotherapist are related to loss or impending loss of a significant interpersonal relationship and threats to financial security or general job satisfaction.

Other values that serve as sources of conflict are in the areas of sex and morality. Although much less so than in Freud's time, sex remains an anxiety-laden topic, especially in Western culture. With the rise of the religious right has come an increased emphasis on the application of moral principles to sexual values and behavior. Sex is thought of less as a communicative tool in our culture than one requiring a moral valence.

Sex is a dominant force in adolescent psychology. Adolescence is a time of hormonal changes, and a great deal of energy is channeled into sexual fantasy and sexual gratification. However, these hormonal changes are probably less important than the relational imperatives that accompany adolescent sexual development. Sexual desire provides much of the motivation for the achievement of these tasks. In our culture, these relational tasks and developmental chores are suppressed in campaigns to encourage abstinence from all types of sexual gratification, including masturbation, in young people by subtly vilifying sexuality. This is not to argue that adolescents need to be having sex. Clearly, the vast majority of adolescents are not able to understand fully the multiple ramifications of sexual behavior. However, simply attempting to brand sexuality with a moral label and demanding that young people refrain from being motivated by sexual longings dismisses the important evocative aspects of relational development that spring from adolescent sexuality.

In my practice, I work with a large number of gay men who struggle with issues related to guilt due to the moral labeling of sexual desire and behavior. However, this area is not the sole province of gay men or lesbians. Many, if not most, of the clients I have worked with in psychotherapy struggle with where sexuality fits into their lives.

Obviously money and sex are two important values in our particular culture. However, there are a multitude of others, too many to explore at any length here. In terms of values, the psychotherapist has two general tasks: to aid the client in identifying those values that are being expressed, either consciously and directly or unconsciously and symbolically, and to aid him or her in evaluating the ongoing utility and applicability of these values and, if necessary, constructing values more in keeping with her or his life's trajectory.

MORTALITY

Closely related to values and meaning in life is the issue of human mortality. Deciding what it means that life is finite is one of the most intimate and complicated of human struggles. Existential psychotherapists have long been aware that one of the primary tasks of therapy is to aid clients in the recognition of ways that they suppress their fear of death and its ultimate shadow across their lives (Becker, 1973; Yalom, 1980). Mortality also figured prominently in Freud's early work regarding the death instinct, *thanatos*, and was much discussed among his early disciples (Ellenberger, 1970). Indeed, Ellenberger proposes that, following the rich philosophical tradition of Hobbes, Schopenhauer, and Nietzsche, Freud asserted that "the goal of life is death" (p. 513). However, Freud argued for the importance, at times the primacy, of the death instinct from a rationalistic biological foundation. He viewed death as part of the logical progression of evolution. The biological underpinnings of this aspect of his theory did not bear up under close scrutiny, even to devoted disciples. A distinction was offered regarding death as the completion of life but not its meaning (Ellenberger, 1970). The emphasis on death in psychoanalytic theory ultimately came to be seen as a biological oversimplification and was first discounted in importance and then basically ignored. Like much of the biologically oriented rationalism of early psychoanalytic theory, there is much to be questioned in the concept of *thanatos*; however, it is ultimately undeniable that mortality has an immense influence on human development and the conduct of life. The systematic avoidance of this topic within much of the mainstream mental health clinical literature mirrors the culture's discomfort with it. More than simply mirroring it, however, the lack of intensive focus on the multiple meanings of mortality in human psychological functioning has served as a means of reinforcing our culture's fear of looking at the issue.

No therapist who has ever worked with a client who has a life-threatening illness, whether it be cancer, heart disease, or AIDS, can come away from the experience without a clear understanding of the centrality that mortality assumes in our psyches. Although most of us spend our days and nights attempting to avoid contemplating what it may mean that we die, this is a central motivation for many of our feelings, thoughts, and behaviors.

One of the ways that I have worked with clients around this issue is to aid them in becoming consciously aware of its existence. Most of us have little control over that which we keep out of our conscious awareness. Especially in working with those with life-threatening illnesses, it is helpful to bring the issue of mortality into sharp relief so that the client can understand the many symbolic and actual consequences of choices and behaviors. I invite clients to think about their thoughts and feelings when they are awake late at night, in bed in the darkness, and feeling alone. For most of us, this image carries with it some sadness and anxiety. These seem to be inevitable parts of the realization of mortality. However, we strive diligently, albeit ineffectively, to stifle these feelings in looking at our lives. This effort to avoid and deny the realization of mortality can lead to many interpersonal and intrapsychic difficulties.

Sam was a paramedic in his late twenties when he began psychotherapy. He complained of two primary difficulties when he presented for treatment. The first was a long-standing difficulty in maintaining intimate, romantic relationships. A handsome man, Sam could easily engage partners for sexual liaisons but had great difficulty maintaining interest in the person after a few sexual encounters. Although he consciously asserted a desire to have a committed relationship, he seemed unable to put this desire into effect. The second difficulty concerned his belief that he should be "doing better" with his career. His parents had wanted him to be a physician, and he clearly had the intelligence and other resources to have accomplished this. Indeed, he had completed his first year of medical school with high marks; however, for reasons he could not entirely articulate, other than to say that "it just didn't feel right," he had dropped out. When he began therapy, he believed that being a physician was "the right thing" for him, but he seemed unable to muster the discipline to return to school.

I tentatively conceptualized his interpersonal and career paralysis as related in some way to a rebellion or disidentification with his parents. Gradually this hypothesis evolved into one that emphasized narcissistic elements (e.g., the fear of success, difficulty tolerating accomplishment and pride). Then, a few months into our work, another possibility asserted itself.

Sam arrived for his regular session appearing calm. He remarked, matter-of-factly and without any discernible emotion, that he had almost missed the appointment because he had been working an auto accident with several fatalities. Reacting without much thought I remarked that this must be an emotionally difficult, even frightening, part of his work. He assured me, in the same casual tone, that he was accustomed to death and was never fazed by it. Following up on what seemed a remarkable emotional position, I challenged his assertion that he was "never" distressed. As the session progressed, it became obvious that Sam's emotional distance from death and life-threatening injury was more than professional hardening.

Over the next few months, Sam and I talked extensively about his emotional reaction—or conscious lack thereof—to death. He seemed bewildered that I would find anything noteworthy about his detachment and dismissed the importance of mortality by stating simply, "Death is unavoidable; it happens to everybody. So why have any feelings about it?" Gradually I challenged this dismissal as being factually, but not necessarily emotionally, accurate. At first, Sam seemed curious as to what feelings one might experience about death. Then he grew more anxious about the topic. I pointed out that this anxiety was probably only the tip of the iceberg.

During one pivotal session, Sam became very sad, and his eyes filled with tears. We were discussing death because he had become more attuned to his emotional distance from the subject and had just worked another accident with a fatality. When I asked why he was feeling sad, he very insightfully acknowledged that he had a sense of why he kept such emotional distance from death.

"If I think about it, nothing would make any sense. Why do anything? Why have anybody? You're just going to lose it all."

"It sounds as if you have already been thinking about it, at least on some level," I suggested.

He looked puzzled and asked what I meant. We talked about the fact that what had brought him to therapy were exactly those issues. He seemed thoughtful and offered, "I'm minimizing my losses." This seemed to sum up Sam's dilemma in a nutshell. He feared availing himself of some of the deepest joys in life because he feared ultimately losing them. This theme was the central one of Sam's therapy. Over the two plus years of our work, we addressed it in many direct and symbolic forms.

When Sam finished his therapy, he was involved in a relationship. There were still moments when this frightened him because he knew it would end; however, he had come to the time-honored conclusion that in order to live, one must be prepared to die. He decided against returning to medical school and instead was pursuing graduate study in philosophy, with the goal of teaching. Although Sam and I ranged over many emotional, psychological, and spiritual areas, I have no doubt that the one that unlocked the most doors for him involved looking at his feelings regarding death and the lengths that he went to in denying them.

ORGANIZATION AND GUIDANCE OF THE UNIVERSE

Closely allied with the creation of meaning in mortality is the creation of meaning regarding the organization of the universe. Whether it be considered a god or some other fundamental element, most of us have some conception of the principles on which the universe is founded. Equally common is a tendency to avoid looking at this idiosyncratic conception and to discount its importance in our characteristic emotional, interpersonal, and cognitive responses.

A client's cosmology can be extremely important in understanding patterns of response to both internal and external stimuli. For instance, if one believes that the universe operates on karma, then one's actions are ostensibly motivated by the desire to increase positive karma and decrease negative karma. If one believes that the universe operates on the whims of an arbitrary god, then one is left at the mercy of an essentially unfathomable set of rules and expectations. If one is influenced by the philosophy that the universe is run strictly on the basis of scientific rules, then one's expectations of mystery and surprise are affected.

Many of our clients do not consider their conception of the organization of the universe to be an important area for exploration; however, they are constantly reacting to this particular conceptualization. As will be considered in the next chapter, many clients operate on the notion, which has been influenced by parental expectations and reactions, that some type of god controls the universe. This is often seen most clearly in psychotherapy when a client is on the path to making substantive and significant changes in life. These changes often go against the grain of what are generally unconscious universal expectations. For instance, a client who expects the universe to be organized around betrayal because that became a pattern in previous relationships will find it quite disturbing when a relationship does not consist of betrayal.

It is equally important that a client recognize that a conception of the universe as essentially having no guiding principles is an understanding of the organization of the universe and its guiding principles. Failure to explore this leaves an important area obscured in the client's understanding of how he or she fits into the larger scheme of the universe.

Gene is an example of such a client. A man in his mid-thirties, Gene presented for psychotherapy wanting to explore a pattern of chaotic romantic relationships, most of which ultimately ended in his being abandoned. During our first session, I was struck by his awareness of this pattern but his almost complete lack of curiosity regarding its foundation.

I began with the premise that Gene's familial relationships were chaotic and injurious. My psychoanalytic background almost invariably suggests family dynamics as the first explanation for recurrent adult relationship patterns. Such early relationships are generally fertile ground that yields much understanding of a client. Further, understanding these patterns often allows a client to recognize their replication in adult relationships more easily and make conscious efforts to change them. This did not happen with Gene.

Over the first months of his therapy, we explored his family extensively. He was a cooperative, even industrious, client, who arrived for each session prepared and willing to talk about the material that I had obviously communicated to him was of most interest to me. However, even given his cooperation and participation, I continued to be struck by his lack of curiosity. He could make connections between past and current relationships, but this understanding seemed to yield no change in the choices he made or the manner in which he conceptualized events.

I first attempted to ascertain whether I had failed to create the safety in our relationship that would allow his making changes. After some exploration of this issue, it seemed that this was not a difficulty, although I did learn how much I was communicating my wish that he be different, an understanding that offered another avenue of exploration. Perhaps we were re-creating the pattern he had originally identified as distressing to him. It *was* feeling a little chaotic; I was engaged in a type of encounter with Gene that I do not find particularly helpful. In some important ways this was a rejection. On one level he perhaps expected that if he continued not to change, I would indeed abandon him. As we discussed this, it did seem to offer a partial explanation of what was transpiring between us. However, there was still a large portion missing from the equation.

I decided in one session simply to comment on the element that had been most striking in our interactions: his lack of curiosity. His response was thoughtful but characteristic. This was indeed the case, but he did not find that particularly noteworthy. I asked why this did not seem noteworthy to him.

"Why should it?" he asked a little defensively. "You can't figure it out anyway."

I first addressed what seemed a narcissistic injury. "It seems as if I may have come across as if I was scolding or demanding that you be curious." Gene relaxed a bit. Then I continued, "I do think it might be important to understand more about your view that things can't be figured out anyway."

There was a moment of puzzlement, followed by a moment of contemplation. Finally, he responded, "Because that's the way it's set up. We've got no control, and we're not supposed to understand the rules."

I was struck by the clarity of his answer, and some important aspects of his worldview became clear. Gene's conception of relationships as chaotic extended to his general cosmology. I had begun where many therapists, especially psychodynamically oriented therapists, begin: that everything about his functioning, especially in terms of relationships, could be understood by understanding early familial relationships.

What I learned as I moved beyond this position, however, was that there was much more to Gene's universe than relationships. Without discounting the enormous power of relationships in developing his cosmology, it was important that we explore the meaning he assigned to nonrelational experiences. The crucial difference was that his understanding of the universe as being chaotically organized influenced his perception of impersonal and random events, as well as that of relationships.

As this aspect of his cosmology unfolded, it became obvious that Gene believed there to be nothing that he could invest with trust as having predictable reactions. His understanding of relationships followed this view in many ways rather than preceding it. His fundamental belief that there was no set of principles that could predict success or failure colored most aspects of his life. With the opening of this new avenue came movement for Gene. It was only in exploring and understanding Gene's cosmology with him that he began to be curious, a prerequisite to change.

SUFFERING

It would be impossible to explore spirituality without taking into account suffering as a human dilemma. Many attempts have been made to account for suffering. However, like most of the other mysteries of life, there is no way to account fully for it. Why is good fortune visited on one individual and ill fortune on another? Why can one person experience robust health throughout life while another is sickly?

Theologians throughout history have grappled with this issue. In many ways it is the linchpin of a comprehensive theology, and a variety of theological positions have been put forward to account for suffering. The Book of Job is an early attempt that has influenced much subsequent Judeo-Christian theology. As traditionally understood, the story of Job is that of a human being tested by an arbitrary god (Kushner, 1981). Job's god tests his willingness to remain faithful, even after being subjected to terrible losses, physical maladies, and other traumata. Ultimately Job passes his god's test and is rewarded with more interpersonally and materially than he originally had lost. This text seems initially to attempt a representation of the inexplicable nature of suffering, but then culminates in a simplistic formula of suffering as related to righteousness. Although it acknowledges that the righteous may suffer, it ultimately holds out the promise that suffering, if conducted righteously, will afford one a closer, more abundant relationship with God. Christian theologians seized on the equation coupling degrees of righteousness with degrees of suffering. Probably best articulated by Augustine, the traditional Christian theological understanding of suffering is that it is the product of sin. Without human sin, there would be no suffering. It was not a distant travel to the even more simplistic notion of suffering that pervades much fundamentalist Protestant theology: one suffers in proportion to one's sinfulness or distance from God's moral principles. This notion accounts for some of the more barbarous suffering we promulgate on each other through the shaming of one who is suffering (e.g., "AIDS is God's punishment for sin").

Some recent theologians (e.g., Kushner, 1981, 1996) have proposed profound challenges to the equation of suffering with sin. These challenges have been greeted with much enthusiasm, but the prevailing dogma available to most people looking for an understanding of suffering is that it is related to one's conduct or essential personal worth, or both.

Interestingly, Eastern religions, most notably Buddhism, have a similar cosmology, albeit somewhat subtler. Through the idea of karma, an explanation of suffering is offered that relates it to one's internal and external conduct. Anger, hate, and the fantasies and behavior that can result from them predispose one to the development of a karma that facilitates suffering.

Just as it questioned many other Christian doctrines, the Western Enlightenment challenged the traditional conception of suffering (May, 1976). Enlightenment philosophers proposed that suffering is ultimately not a mystery. Rather, it is understandable as a natural consequence of immutable physical laws—what Thomas Carlyle labeled "natural supernaturalism." The fact that it seems a mystery can be accounted for by the fact that we do not yet understand all the laws governing the universe.

The rationalism of the Enlightenment deeply influenced Freud's early psychoanalytic theories. He presented at least a portion of the mystery of suffering as completely understandable in psychological terms. Much human suffering is brought about through the unconscious direction of behavior. *Thanatos* was the first explanation for the motivation driving intrapsychic and interpersonal behavior that results in suffering. As *thanatos* was discounted as an important human motivation, the superego became a more sophisticated focus. The superego demands retribution for violations of its prescriptions and proscriptions, and this retribution results in internal and external suffering. Currently, the primary psychodynamic conception of suffering is masochism. Masochism remains a popular, although controversial, psychological explanation for much suffering. Ultimately, psychodynamic theory has come to the same conclusion as theology: we bring much of our own suffering upon ourselves.

The twentieth century has seen the medicalization of Western culture. The Western conception, especially of physical suffering, has evolved to include genetics, chemistry, and other sciences, but it offers no definitive explanation of the randomness of even physical difficulties. Like all explanations, it covers only a portion of the question asked by the dilemma of suffering.

Although I recognize a certain oversimplification of some very complex theological, philosophical, and psychological theories, I do so to make the point that the conception of suffering as retribution pervades much of Western culture and deeply influences many clients' perceptions of their own suffering. This is not to argue that there are no clients who come for psychotherapy wishing to blame their suffering on other factors. Indeed, in this era of easy victimization, many clients are determined to find a facile external focus for their suffering. Both positions, however, are subject to the same flaw: they equate suffering with wronging or being wronged, and they too easily dismiss the mystery of suffering, offering instead facile answers. One common focus of a spiritually attuned psychotherapy experience is the exploration of the mystery of suffering. The therapist often challenges the client's conception of suffering, not to argue her or him out of it but to create an understanding of suffering that respects its unwillingness to be explained easily and completely. This was the case with Ann.

Ann, a woman in her late forties, presented for therapy with a debilitating neurological disease that caused her great physical distress and interfered with her ability to accomplish routine daily activities. Before her illness, she had been active and athletic and she had prided herself not only on her physical competence but on her independence. Her illness robbed her of both capacities. As she found her physical capacities diminished, she was increasingly dependent on family and friends. She was ambivalent about this dependence at best and hostile at worst. From the outset of therapy, she expressed resentment of friends and family members not afflicted, but also guilt that she experienced these feelings toward them. She wondered aloud why she had merited such a painful and debilitating disease, and we devoted many hours of her therapy to looking at her understanding of this phenomenon.

Ann saw suffering as a punishment for hitherto unrecognized sins, especially her envious and jealous feelings of childhood. Ann had two younger siblings, a brother and a sister. As is often the case with the firstborn, Ann's parents had been somewhat stricter with her than with her siblings, and throughout her childhood, she had resented her siblings for their easier path in life. Her parents reacted strongly to Ann's feelings, chastising her regularly for being resentful or envious. Although apparently not religious, Ann's parents seemed to find resentment an especially heinous sin and often told her that she would be punished for this feeling. The first task of our work together was to clarify the relationship for her between punishment and suffering, not because it would necessarily change the feelings involved but because it offered her an understanding of some of her reactions.

One of the most helpful things that therapy can do with regard to spirituality is not to change a client's view but to amplify it or bring it into sharper focus so that the client may scrutinize it more carefully and decide whether it truly fits the individual circumstances of life. In regard to suffering, it can also be helpful for the therapist to introduce the role of mystery in suffering. Several months into therapy, Ann still saw suffering, especially her suffering, as a result of sin. I never challenged this view directly because I had nothing any more definitive with which to replace it. However, I did challenge the completeness of her view. As she would acknowledge her belief that she was being punished for old and new sins, I would question.

During one session, she was in an unusual amount of pain and sobbed in despair, "Why do I do this to myself?"

Frustrated, I asked, "What are you doing to yourself?"

"Godammit, we've talked about all this before! I can't let go of my negative feelings. If I could, I could heal myself, but I can't!"

"Who says?" I queried.

"What?" she demanded, clearly frustrated with me.

"Okay, where is it written that if you could rid yourself of 'negative' feelings, you could be healed?"

"Everywhere!" she practically screamed. "The seven deadly sins, Norman fucking Vincent Peale, Bernie Siegel, you name it!"

"So they've got the answer?" I challenged.

At that moment Ann broke into a sheepish laughter. "No, of course not. But they do have *something* there," she asserted, regaining a sense of seriousness.

"No doubt," I retreated, "But . . ."

"But maybe I'm making this too easy," she proposed.

I was surprised that from this interchange she had understood a central point I had been offering for months. However, part of the excitement of psychotherapy remains the surprise in seeing the multiple and sometimes incomprehensible ways that clients have of reaching conclusions.

This is not to say that Ann's view of her suffering and its genesis changed completely, or even dramatically, as a result of this interchange or the dozens previous to it. She still generally held to the notion that suffering was the result of the inability to master "negative" feelings. What did change was her absolute conviction in this. She now allowed herself room for doubt and as a result was able to hold an internal dialogue with herself about this view as it applied to her particular situation. While obviously not providing any real physical comfort, this eased the guilt that seemed to exacerbate her pain. Further, it offered her the opportunity to talk with family members about her feelings, of which she was no longer ashamed. Once this process began, she was amazed that she was not alone in her "negative" feelings; her family shared some of them, and they even felt some of them toward her. Paradoxically, this provided much relief to her. By the time we terminated, she reportedly felt much more comfortable relying on her family and friends for support and, although I doubt that there was any physiological basis for it, some diminution of her physical distress. In my estimation, her willingness to tolerate some mystery in her conception of suffering played a key role in this outcome.

TRANSCENDENCE

Finally, the sixth element involved in an understanding of spirituality concerns what, if anything, takes place after death. This I refer to as transcendence. Use of this word is somewhat biased in that it suggests that *something* happens after death—that we transcend. Such may not be the case. Nevertheless, most of us nurture a belief that something happens after death, even if it is simply the cessation of consciousness and the deterioration of the body. This idea motivates and guides much of an individual's feelings, fantasies, and behavior. For instance, someone who believes that heaven or hell awaits after death ostensibly attempts to gain the former and avoid the latter. Someone who believes that reincarnation awaits contemplates what lessons are to be learned in this life. As in the case of suffering, this is one of the ultimate mysteries of life, and there is no definitive answer to it. However, aiding clients in exploring their views of transcendence better equips them to hold internal dialogues about their views and expand, change, or otherwise modify them if they do not fit or they interfere with other life circumstances. As is the case with suffering, offering the client the idea that mystery is an inextricable part of the end of life both arouses anxiety and offers comfort.

One of the faults Freud (1927, 1939) found with organized religion, echoed by contemporary existential psychotherapists like Yalom (1980), is that it attempts to deny the finality of death. Freud's critique centers on that aspect of organized Judeo-Christian religion that seems to propose that after death we go on as before, only, optimally, better. If in God's favor, we transcend earthly existence and achieve paradise. If out of favor, we take up residence in purgatory (or hell, or sheol, or somewhere else). Ultimately, in either case, Freud argued, we avoid experiencing the anxiety of ending by believing that we simply cross a border (Gay, 1989a).

Like most of the rest of his thinking, there is a profound resonance to Freud's thinking in this area. One has only to listen to any of the Protestant television evangelists to hear simplistic ideas proposed regarding events after death. Reacting to this, one of my clients asserted during a session, "I don't want to be in God's choir and sing all day long. Boring!" However, there is a darker side to this dilemma than whether one wishes to be a tenor in the celestial choir.

Many clients, especially those raised in more conservative Christian (whether Catholic or Protestant) environments, live in the shadow of damnation. Where Freud seems to have been overly simplistic in his view of organized religion as neurotically protecting human beings from the anxiety surrounding death is in this area. The threat of damnation is real and ever present for many clients. More anxiety has probably been aroused by organized religion than has been neurotically suppressed. It is to this suffering that spiritually attuned psychotherapy best addresses itself. However, to be optimally authentic, it must again respect the mystery of transcendence.

As with the dilemma of suffering, one important set of goals for psychotherapy is to determine a client's beliefs in this area and help to explore them—not with the goal of replacing "faulty" beliefs but to open the door to mystery. Psychotherapists have no more idea of what happens after death than anyone else; we cannot offer definitive answers. Nevertheless, we can offer clients a companion in fully exploring and questioning their beliefs. In this process some beliefs may grow stronger while others diminish. After such exploration, what typically remains is a client's authentic, integrated view of transcendence that, because it is authentic, will be a source of support for other aspects of a spiritual perspective and identity. This process can be illustrated through discussion of my work with Ben, a gay professional man in his mid-twenties.

Ben ostensibly sought out psychotherapy because of dilemmas he was experiencing in his career as a successful health care professional, working at a large metropolitan hospital. He related that colleagues valued him and he was generally quite popular at work. However, he felt ambivalent about his work and believed that he could be doing something more fulfilling.

He typically related information in a low monotone and with little enthusiasm. As we discussed other areas of his life, he reported having no primary romantic partner but dated casually. He denied ever having any long-term relationships. He described his original family as "strict but supportive." He had been brought up in the Catholic church but described himself as not currently very devout.

As is generally the case when a client presents one problem as being the focus of his difficulties, while another, more important, lies just beneath the surface, Ben was unable to give much detail regarding his lack of work satisfaction. When I would ask for more specificity regarding how his work might be more fulfilling, he would merely shrug and say, "You know, I could be getting more out of it." At these times it is apparent that whatever the fundamental difficulty is will be brought out at its own pace, and so I sit back and wait for developments.

As time progressed, Ben talked less about his work situation and more about his family. He was not yet "out" to his family and feared their reaction when they discovered his homosexuality. The monotonous quality of his voice was replaced at these times by a quality that suggested vague terror. I commented on that to him at one point, and he acknowledged a deep fear that they would reject him if they were to discover it. He related that their viewpoint was linked with their religious convictions, and, more matter-of-factly than at any point thus far in the conversation, he noted "something to do with not consorting with the damned."

"Consorting with the damned?" I asked with more than a little surprise.

He sat impassively, nodding that I had indeed understood him. Ben went on to explain that he did not necessarily believe that he was damned, but that this sometimes was a source of some frightening internal speculation.

As we continued to work together, this aspect of his internal world became more prominent. He had taken the particular job he had because it was a way to bargain with God. He was helping other people, which might balance out, at least to some extent, the damnable offense of being gay; however, he resented having to do something that, although apparently quite good at, he did not enjoy.

About nine months into his therapy, Ben arrived for one session very angry. I inquired as to the reason, because it was an anomaly in my experience with him. "It's this book I'm reading," he responded.

"What are you reading?"

"That book by John Boswell about same-sex marriages [1994]," he responded with a contemptuous hiss.

"That's made you angry?" I asked, curious as to what was happening.

"How dare he turn everything around! Okay, so maybe we can't help being gay, but that doesn't mean that it's fine with God. The Scriptures are very clear on it. He can't just claim that church writings and tradition say something they don't." Ben's face was red, and he was clearly enraged.

Knowing that I would be wading in with crocodiles, I asked, "You don't think it's open to interpretation?"

"No, I don't," he responded dismissively.

"Then what accounts for its bothering you so much?"

"The lies. That's what bothers me so much," he said somewhat more timidly.

"If they're just lies, why not just ignore them?" I responded.

Ben looked perplexed.

"Maybe this isn't as easy as truth versus lies," I suggested. "Maybe that's why you're angry."

"So," he began with irritation, "dazzle me with an insight."

"No insight. That's the point. Perhaps nobody really knows how God feels about homosexuality. Perhaps that's a mystery that allows different interpretations."

"Next, you'll tell me that there's no assurance homosexuals will be sent to hell." While challenging, Ben's look also betrayed some hope.

"In my mind, there's no assurance of that. I would not order my life around that as a certainty."

"Like I've done," he offered, appearing genuinely thoughtful.

Ben's is an example of multiple clinical phenomena (splitting, internalized homophobia, etc.). Most important for this discussion, however, it is an example of the importance that transcendence plays in a spiritual perspective. Ben ordered much of his life around the idea that he would be banished to hell after death. An important part of his therapy was simply opening the possibility of mystery in this area. Once this was genuinely done, after multiple interchanges like the one above, he made a number of significant changes in his life, including getting a new job that offered more to him personally.

CONCLUSION

Obviously, this list of spiritual elements is not exhaustive, but I have found it to be most helpful in organizing my work with clients in terms of the spiritual dimensions of their lives. In contradistinction to our current understanding of psychotherapy, the goal is not to change a client's beliefs about a particular aspect of this system. Indeed, psychotherapy is not really about change. Instead, psychotherapy, especially in the spiritual realm, where few true answers can be achieved and externally imposed, must focus on illuminating the path on which the client is moving and offering options that will allow the client to see other potential paths. This process is constructive in nature and can build only on elements available to the client. Therefore, the imposition of a particular spiritual perspective is almost certainly bound to fail. Although a client may give conscious acknowledgment of it and even allegiance to it, such a perspective will probably not take root if it does not fit with the client's spiritual foundation. This brings us to the earliest influence on the spiritual dimension: parents.

CHAPTER THREE

THE ROLE OF PARENTS IN SPIRITUAL DEVELOPMENT

Reducing the entirety of spirituality to identifications with parents is an oversimplification, yet it is impossible to consider spirituality without looking at the role that parents and identifications with them play in its development. In this chapter, discussion will be undertaken of the pivotal role that parents play in the initiation and maintenance of a spiritual outlook. Specific emphasis will be placed on some types of spiritual perspective that are often seen in clinical practice and relate directly to identifications with parents.

"Our Father, who is in Heaven," begins the central prayer of Christianity. It emphasizes the direct connection between God and the human father. Recent attempts to depaternalize the language of this particular prayer have changed it to "Our Mother" and "Our Parent," yet all these revisions continue to emphasize God as parent.

Other monotheistic faiths—those that emphasize a concept of God open to human anthropomorphization—do likewise. The Old Testament, for instance, clearly depicts God as a father to Israel. God is reported to feel most of the feelings that a father would feel and takes many of the actions, based on those feelings, that a father would be expected to take. Islam as well places Allah in the role of a holy father. It is only the Eastern religions in which this analogy breaks down to some extent. Since many of these religions, especially Buddhism, do not emphasize a monotheistic understanding of the universe, there is not a readily apparent correlation with a parental god. However, in these spiritual systems, the child's tendency to equate the ultimate force guiding the universe with parents is almost unavoidable.

THE ROLE OF DEPENDENCE IN SPIRITUAL DEVELOPMENT

A newborn baby is almost totally devoid of the ability to care for itself. It is completely at the mercy of caregivers as to whether it flourishes, finds satisfaction, or even survives. Mahler and those influenced by her work (Mahler, Pine, & Bergman, 1975) have argued that, at least for the first months of life, the baby is not psychologically differentiated from its mother and therefore does not recognize its utter dependence. More recent infant research (principally Stern, 1985) has challenged that particular perspective. Indeed, it appears that from virtually the first few hours after birth, the baby recognizes itself to be an entity apart from mother, although defining exact boundaries will be the work of many months. If this view is accurate, then the baby is aware to some extent of its complete dependence on parents almost from birth. However, even if Mahler's thinking is accurate, after the first few months of life, the baby certainly becomes aware of its total dependence for life on parents, most especially its mother.

It is in this realization of total dependence that the initial correlation of parents and spirituality occurs. The baby has little option but to see its parents as godlike, holding absolute power of life and death. The infant is entirely dependent on parents for the essentials of life: food, shelter, and protection. Equally important, as Spitz's (1965) research highlighted, parents provide emotional sustenance to the baby. While imperative to future psychological development, the emotional ambiance created by primary caregivers has immediate, tangible, and significant physical ramifications for the baby. An ambiance of sterility, coldness, or frank hatred can endanger the infant's life. The withholding of love may literally result in the baby's death.

If parents provide enough for the baby to survive, the child carries throughout development the imprints of the feelings aroused in this experience of dependence. Most important, the person carries throughout life a sense of whether there was enough. Was there enough food? Was there enough responsiveness to moments of distress? Was there enough physical contact? In short, was there enough love? Kushner (1996) argues that it is the experience of the amount and availability of love that influences much later spiritual development. If, in utter dependence, the baby experiences the parents—the whole of its universe—as having enough love to share and sharing that love, the child will have little difficulty developing a spiritual perspective that includes a belief that the universe holds enough love to share among its many diverse inhabitants. If the baby experiences its parents as not having enough love to share with it, then the universe similarly becomes organized around the idea that there is not enough to go around: not enough money, not enough fame, not enough praise—above all, not enough love. Among the monotheistic religions, which tend to personalize their god, it is quite easy for a developing child to see in her or his god the same capacity to experience and share love as characterized parents.

Later cognitive teaching about spiritual and religious beliefs may attempt to supplant this notion. For instance, Christianity argues that God is not human but instead is perfect, while parents are human and therefore imperfect. The Christian god is not susceptible to the difficulties that can hinder human parents. Even if the parents were unable to give the child what was needed, God, it is argued, can. Christian theology argues that its god is all-loving. Unfortunately, Christian practice more often resembles a parent, limited in the capacity to love. The result, especially among more conservative Christian groups, is a set of mystifying teachings. God is supposedly a being of love and light—unless you do not conform to the particular teachings of that group or you belong to a group, like homosexuals, "humanists," or atheists, who are willfully disobedient and therefore beyond love. For some Christian groups, hell is an ever-present danger. One can be consigned to its eternal agonies for multiple transgressions, including those that are an inescapable part of being human, such as anger and lust. Perhaps more important, one can be damned for what are arguably quite healthy characteristics, including the capacity to feel pride (e.g., "Pride goeth before a fall").

Many Eastern religions do away with a central god entirely and focus the child's attention on concepts such as karma and nirvana, which tend to be less personalized. (Interestingly, though, in Buddhism, as in the case of most other Eastern religions, there are figures who can be compared to parents. The Buddha, or Buddhas, serve such a purpose.) Even under the best of circumstances, the cognitive retraining by religions is never as powerful as the experiential training of being totally dependent on parents, completely at the mercy of another being. Therefore, throughout life, each of us carries a conceptualization of the motivating force of the universe as being akin to our parents. This does not suggest that identifications with parents form the sole context of a spiritual perspective; however, it suggests that understanding a client's early interactions with parents helps in understanding that client's spiritual perspective.

PARENTS AND SPIRITUAL HUNGER

While most psychotherapists are accustomed to exploring a client's relationships with parents as a means of understanding current interpersonal, affective, and thought patterns, there is less comfort and sense of custom in exploring the relationship with parents to understand a client's spiritual adaptation. Partly this is related to a general avoidance of the topic of spirituality in clinical work. Nevertheless, it is important to begin to think in terms of a client's spiritual development as originating in the primary dependence that that client experienced on parents or primary caregivers. This understanding will begin to offer insight into the foundation on which the client has attempted to build a cognitive and affective understanding of the universe and her or his spiritual place in it. Some authors (e.g., Hillman, 1996) have challenged the bedrock psychodynamic contention that the seeds of most adult functioning are sown in interactions with parents. Especially among psychotherapists attuned to the spiritual dimension, the role of parents in shaping later spiritual adaptation has been questioned. Jung, the first systematic theorist to deal with spirituality, discounted the role of parents through belief that a considerable amount of functioning, especially in the spiritual realm, was influenced by archetypes and the collective unconscious. Although Jung never negated the effect that parents have on the developing child's spiritual perspective, he afforded equal weight to less idiosyncratic factors like archetypal influences.

Contemporary archetypal therapists have continued to attempt to balance the role of parents with that of more socially and psychologically intrinsic factors. Hillman (1996), for instance, argues that it is the child, born with a particular daemon or guiding spirit, who picks parents who will fulfill a particular destiny. This platonic idea completely reverses the traditional dynamic conception of development. According to it, the child enters the world with a preordained destiny to fulfill. Rather than parents', or for that matter culture's, shaping the child's developmental course, the child's destiny determines the particular parents and culture into which that child will be born and grow.

Although there has perhaps been too much emphasis placed on the role that parents play in the development of most facets of a child's life, it seems equally erroneous to assert that parents are superfluous to the development of spirituality. While Hillman offers intriguing examples, especially from the history of the arts, to support his contention, most clients who seek psychotherapeutic aid to resolve difficulties in their spirituality offer abundant evidence that parents and the environment they create have a profound impact on the course of spiritual development. Two common clinical presentations can generally be traced to the impact of parents on the child during development, but especially during periods of complete dependency.

THE NARCISSISTIC GOD

Jane was a successful professional woman in her late twenties when we began working together. Initially she described her difficulties as involving depression coupled with intense anxiety related to professional achievements, an inability to maintain long-term relationships, and a general sense of loneliness and emptiness in her life. She complained most bitterly about a sense that "nothing was ever good enough" for those with whom she was in relationships. With a little exploration, it became clear that much of her depression was fueled by a sense of not being "good enough" in any setting. She worked strenuous hours, demanded perfection of herself in all activities, and was unmercifully critical if she fell short of what often seemed superhuman goals.

Jane's spirituality was a dilemma equal to any other in her life, although she was initially embarrassed to admit to such a quandary ("That doesn't really seem to go with the twentieth century," she offered at one point). Ultimately she was deeply distressed by her sense that on a cosmic scale, as on the more personal, she did not measure up. When we began exploring her spiritual perspective, it was very much an intellectual perspective consisting of a mix of Eastern and Western philosophical and theological tenets. The only aspect of her perspective that seemed emotionally integrated was her belief that she was placed on earth with a particular mission, which involved improving others' lives.

Jane had been raised in a conservative Protestant church that demanded that a number of articles of its doctrine be taken on faith— without question. Early in our work together, we began to understand her initial dismissal of spirituality as medieval or primitive as related to this idea of not questioning basic religious tenets.

The god of Jane's early religious training was especially important in understanding her confusion and superhuman expectations of herself. "He was the God of original sin," she asserted. In her conception, nothing she could ever do would be enough to please him. He demanded perfection. God, after all, knew the secret feelings and desires that she hid from others, and often from herself. He was constantly displeased with her, although as an adult she dealt with this through her intellectual dismissal of his importance and her mixture of philosophies. She remembered in her early church experiences the constant admonition that "God will forgive you if you only ask." The difficulty was that Jane could never quite understand, as either a child or an adult, exactly what it was for which she should be constantly seeking forgiveness.

The most common clinical manifestation of spiritual difficulty that I encounter in my practice is that of the narcissistic god, who typically demands absolute obedience from his human subjects, is rarely, if ever, satisfied, and often takes credit for all human endeavors. To some extent, this is the god described in the Old and New Testaments, as interpreted by modern Christianity. It was Jane's god.

The narcissistic god demands that his followers continually worship and fear him, and he demands as well that his supplicants continually acknowledge their unworthiness of his love, appreciation, or concern. With the advent of original sin in the work of St. Augustine, this particular god was given special impetus. Like all other things religious, the god created by medieval Europe is understandable in historical context but, if taken literally, creates much turmoil in the modern world.

Augustine's pessimistic god was born in the disappointment and disillusionment that followed the sacking of Rome, the light of the ancient world, by the barbaric German tribes and the darkness that followed. Augustine's was a god created to explain why the world needed punishment (R. D. Laing, 1995, captures Augustinian pessimism beautifully in his cynical quip that "life is a sexually transmitted disease with a one hundred percent mortality rate"). In the same vein, the god of Thomas Aquinas, arguably the most influential portrait of God save that of Augustine, was born from the need to combat the "heresy" endangering the twelfth- and thirteenth-century Catholic church. A movement within the church, the Cathars, proposed the possibility of living a virtuous and uncorrupted life. Indeed, there were some members of this group, the *perfecti*, who supposedly led untarnished— perfect—lives. Like the Pharisees of the period of Jesus' life, the Cathar *perfecti* attempted to live exemplary lives and rejected behaviors that would endanger their virtuous relationship to their god. For a number of reasons, not the least of which was that the Cathar commitment to virtuous behavior stood in stark contrast to the excesses of the clerical hierarchy, the church mobilized against them through physical persecution. Theologically, the church challenged their contention that perfectly virtuous lives are possible. It was in this realm that Aquinas offered his influential conceptions of good and evil. Aquinas argued that behavior was only part of life (a debate still unsettled in some quarters of psychological theory). Thoughts and feelings, the generally externally unknown, were also important. A "perfect" life was proposed as impossible because we are all not only tainted by original sin, but we continually sin anew in our internal worlds. The god created by Aquinas knows all thoughts and all desires; nothing is hidden from him. No secret remains from Aquinas's god, who, knowing all, is a god of disappointment and disapproval (Stanford, 1996). The gods of Augustine and Aquinas have shaped much Western theology, both Catholic and Protestant.

The parallels between such gods and narcissistic parents are obvious and easily made. Clients whose expectation that their spiritual place in the universe is to be continually rebuffed for not being "good enough" often have parents who are narcissistically hungry, demanding a great deal from their children and giving back very little. Indeed, the relationship between parent and child is often inverted, with the child expected to meet parental needs for affirmation and acknowledgment. Such children, like their parents, grow up hungry for narcissistic gratification. (It should be noted that any reference to narcissism or narcissistic gratification implies no pathological intent. Indeed, as Kohut, 1977, proposed, narcissism is an inherent and ubiquitous part of human development.) This narcissistic hunger often presents itself as a need for overt acknowledgment and affirmation, a jealousy of those who receive such acknowledgment and affirmation, a derision of others when their accomplishments are acknowledged, and a general sense of longing to be seen, understood, and appreciated. Often, at some point in therapy, a client with such a background will allude to a belief that the universe operates on the same principle that her or his family did. Put simply, whether it is expressed as a Christian God, Allah, fate, destiny, or some other force, these clients believe that their needs are never to be met and their sole function in the universe is to supplicate before a higher power.

In the South, where religion is taken somewhat more seriously than in some other parts of the country, it is also quite easy to see the development of a belief in a narcissistic god in "Christian teachings." A great deal of Christianity is built on the idea that a narcissistic god must be appeased. Because of original sin, Christ was sent into the world to be tortured and sacrificed to atone. This teaching is powerful indeed, and many clients in my practice must grapple with this portion of their religious education at some point during their therapy.

About six months into her therapy, Jane began to talk about her spiritual struggles. Although she initially minimized their importance by repeatedly calling them "flaky," she seemed almost desperate to discuss many contradictions that she experienced in her spirituality.

She had already let me know that her parents were demanding people—of themselves and their children. She remembered bringing home report cards that were perfect in all respects save one B in a subject. Her parents immediately focused on that particular subject with "suggestions for how to improve it." Although she never came away from these interactions feeling affirmed for her hard work, she would often assert to me, "That was good. They taught me to always strive for excellence." One important moment came in our work together when I simply asked her, "How will you ever know if you've made it?" and she realized that she had never entertained this possibility.

She also told me about family discussions that emphasized humility (which on one occasion she referred to as "humiliation" in a parapraxis). Her parents continually reminded her, "You have nothing to be proud of. You're no better than anyone else," to which she added, "I often felt *worse* than everybody else." One of her most important memories was of high school graduation. As valedictorian of her class, she delivered a short speech and received a good deal of attention. Afterward she caught up with her parents, who were talking with a group of teachers and other parents. Initially Jane was ecstatic as she witnessed her parents introducing her around the group. Her feeling soon changed to consternation. The first oddity of the situation was that her parents were introducing her to several people she already knew, including some of her teachers. The second initially puzzling aspect was that she was continually introduced as "My daughter." She did not hear her name mentioned once. She realized that the entire ritual had been about her parents, not *her*. After relating this in a session, she cried and said, "I was superfluous."

Against this understanding of her family, her spiritual concerns arose. Her spiritual distress followed much the same pattern as that established with her parents at her graduation. As our work together continued, she began, first intimating and later stating more directly, her belief that her only value to God was in those moments in which she either kneeled down or offered a prayer of thanks when she had accomplished something, thereby giving credit to him. She was convinced that she was of absolutely no value to him in those moments in which she stopped briefly to offer herself congratulations and thereby experience fleeting pride. Often, when discussing her spiritual struggles, we would return to the graduation experience as providing a symbolic explanatory template of her understanding of her god's basic narcissistic limitations.

Not surprisingly, as therapy progressed, there was a direct relationship between her evolving view of her god and her view of her parents. As she began to see her parents' narcissistic limitations, she began to question her conception of God. This, however, created a new dilemma. This new conception of God did not include many of the emotions and actions attributed to him in the Christian Bible. She began to wonder how God could be responsible for so much jealousy, hatred, narcissistic rage, and sacrifice, and ultimately she questioned her adherence to Christianity. Her early spiritual training was called into question, and she had no replacement for it. The vacuum created by this process was powerful, at times overwhelming. The depression that had originally brought her to my office, and had begun to loosen its grip, reasserted itself.

For several months, Jane mourned the loss of her previous intellectual and emotional convictions. Although they had been painful, even crippling, they were familiar, and their loss was deeply painful. Along with this loss of accustomed conviction, she was also losing a view of her parents. Together, these losses were devastating and at times seemingly insurmountable. Jane was experiencing a period of what Myss

(1996) refers to as "spiritual madness." Creation generally springs from such spiritual chaos or madness, and the ability to tolerate chaos is one of the key qualities of a spiritually attuned psychotherapist. If one can tolerate the client's painful chaos, he or she will ultimately find/create something much more complete and syntonic to his or her life and its overall direction.

For Jane, this chaos lasted several months, but out of it ultimately developed a new conception of the ordering of the universe. She was unsure of the existence or meaning of God, but was certain that the god portrayed in the Bible was not a god to whom she felt allegiance. Ultimately she joined a Unitarian congregation in which she felt much more at home than she ever had previously in church. She was pleased and reassured by the fact that her congregation followed "principles" rather than an anthropomorphized version of God. Her growing comfort in her changing psychological and spiritual landscape was reflected in her increasing ability to tolerate pride in her accomplishments and acceptance of ambition as a natural part of her life.

After three years of hard work for both of us, the depression and spiritual malaise that had plagued Jane at the outset of our work had receded, and she reported in its place an increased sense of satisfaction, tranquility, and, perhaps most important, congruity.

THE PUNITIVE GOD

Closely related to the narcissistic god is the punitive god. This manifestation of spirituality involves the belief that one will be punished for certain acts and rewarded for others. Again, the Judeo-Christian tradition is most influenced by this particular idea. This understanding of the spiritual functioning of the universe is often presented in the belief that some people go to heaven while others go to hell. In my practice, clients often attempt to reconcile the conflicted picture they are presented of God: that he is both forgiving and beneficent but also consigns some unrepentant sinners (or those who have not been exposed to Christianity) to hell. They similarly struggle with the confused injunction passed out by many churches that one cannot earn one's way into heaven, that it is a gift of grace. However, this simply does not match with the idea that some will go to hell, again even those not exposed to Christian teachings.

The parallel of this particular picture to parents who are punitive and conditional in their love is also obvious. One need only scratch the surface with a client who has had punitive and conditionally caring parents to discover a deeply held fear of being consigned to hell or some other eternal punishment.

Jake was such a client. Initially presenting himself as cheerful, confident, and in command of every situation, Jake was something of a conundrum. For the first couple of sessions, I could not get a clear sense of why he was seeking psychotherapy. All attempts to engage him in a discussion of potentially troubling areas met with a smile and a short dismissal of distress in that particular area. Ultimately I decided that this approach was not going to accomplish my goal of understanding the difficulties motivating Jake to seek treatment.

In the third session, I simply sat back and decided to get to know Jake. He began to tell me bits of information about his family. His parents were originally described as attentive, loving, and kind—"the best parents I could have had," he asserted with a disingenuous smile, which I noted for later discussion. He described his childhood as idyllic. He had all the toys he wanted and never lacked for anything material. However, he had few friends. When I questioned this, he essentially shrugged it off and said, "Who knows how kids think?"

"Well, I would think it possible that *you* would know how *you* thought," I countered.

"I was just a dumb kid," he argued. "I was just scared that they wouldn't like me."

This seemed intriguing, and I followed it up with a question regarding what might make him unlikeable.

"Oh, who knows where kids get ideas?"

"Sometimes from their parents," I proposed quietly.

"Yeah, I guess so," he remarked noncommittally, yet with a palpable increase in his level of anxiety.

Over a period of several months, Jake began to describe some telling incidents from his family. One of these was a trip that he was not allowed to take with the rest of the family because of "something I did wrong."

"What was that?" I asked.

"I didn't apologize. See, there was this day when I was about five that I wanted to fly my kite. I had just gotten it for my birthday. My mother told me that I couldn't, because it was too windy." (A look of puzzlement on my face became perceptible to him.) "If it was too windy I might lose the kite. Anyway, I got mad."

"Yes?" I offered, expecting to hear of some acting out.

"That was it. I got mad and went to my room."

"You didn't say or do anything?" I asked, still puzzled.

"No, I don't think so," he continued. "My mom just came to my room and told me that I couldn't go to my grandmother's house with them. That was bad, 'cause I really loved my grandmother."

Jake's reticence to describe anything emotionally tinged was beginning to become understandable. "Doesn't that seem overly harsh?" I suggested.

"No. Well, maybe—but not at the time. They explained it to me very clearly. They said that when I did something wrong, I would be punished. In the end, they said that if you do enough wrong, you wind up in hell."

"Yeah, but what you 'did wrong' was experience a human feeling," I asserted.

"Feelings can be just as wrong as anything else," he countered with a force suggesting that this was an unquestionable fact of his family's training.

When I asked him about his spiritual background, he described it with some pride as "fire-and-brimstone Baptist."

As time progressed, Jake revealed deep conflicts about a variety of areas in his life. Most important to him, we began to learn, was a sense that he really did not like people. Perhaps more accurately, he was unsure whether he liked or enjoyed other human beings. Not surprisingly, beneath his affable and confident exterior there lay deep rage, of which he was only partially, and ashamedly, aware.

Gradually Jake began to feel and then talk about his rage and deep ambivalence toward others. As he did so, he grew increasingly anxious, almost at some points resembling a child who has done something for which he knows the world will collapse. During one session, this look was so poignant that I felt obliged to comment on it. Jake immediately reacted as if I had viciously criticized him. He informed me with indignant, enraged vehemence that he could not help it!

"Of course not," I found myself saying reflexively.

There was a stunned silence for a moment, and then, more calmly, he asked me what I meant by this last comment. I explained only that I meant that feelings are just that: something we feel. In my estimation, they carry no moral valence. He looked shocked, then surprised, and then relieved. It was at this point that Jake revealed his first dream.

In the dream, he was standing in an open field. Although the sun shone brightly, he felt vague unease. In the distance, he began to hear thunder. His unease became anxiety and then, as the thunder grew nearer, fear. He began to walk, then run, from the approaching storm, the dark clouds growing darker and the thunder ever nearer. In the distance he saw his parents. At first, they were a welcome, reassuring sight. However, as he grew nearer to them, he began to detect disapproval on their faces. He felt terrified and very alone. Ultimately, as he came within easy view of them, they both raised their hands with fingers pointing accusingly at him. He knew they were thinking that he had done something wrong. Suddenly the storm was upon him, and he felt engulfed and carried away in blackness. At this point he had awakened terrified. The dream had lingered with him the next day like a hangover. At times during that day, he thought about the dream and almost burst into tears.

Jake offered an interpretation of this dream that flowed naturally from this session. He proposed that the dream was about his parents' discomfort with and disapproval of his feelings, especially what they referred to as "dark feelings," like anger. I listened to this, one of the clearest, most concise interpretations of a dream I have yet heard, and was aware that it resonated to my overall thoughts about the dream, this particular session, and our work together thus far. Yet there seemed to be another element to the dream.

"What do you think happened as you were carried off by the storm?" I inquired.

"I don't know. The dream ended there," he responded hesitantly.

"Okay, but looking back on the dream now, what do you think would happen after you were carried off by the storm?"

He was quiet and looked troubled. Then tears began to fill his eyes. He noted quietly "I want to cry, but I'm not sure why." There was a pause that I could not intrude upon. I think we both looked expectantly at each other.

"I was taken off to hell."

Although I was at least partially expecting such an answer, it still seemed like a surreal moment. "Why?" I asked, half-knowing the answer I would get.

"Because I am angry. I hate people. I deserve to be damned!" he stammered. This revelation quickly dissolved into tears.

Over the next several months, Jake and I grew to understand more about the exquisite logic of this response. His parents were terrified of anger. As he fleshed out for me some of their early histories of having been physically abused, this terror made perfect sense. They attempted not to experience their own anger, and they demanded that Jake follow suit. Further, they invested their fear (and hatred) in the feeling of anger rather than the manner in which this had been acted out.

Jake also began to develop a sense of why his parents had been drawn to the religion that obsessed them. The god preached from the pulpit of their church was an angry, punishing god—in a spiritual sense, an abusive parent. They could identify with the aggressor, but do so in the guise of love. The god who consigned people to hell—perhaps the most vehement act of hate imaginable—did so out of love.

As this complex story unfolded, Jake became increasingly sad and desolate. He was not depressed, as he sometimes labeled it. Depression is the intense attempt not to feel something, especially anger. Jake was surrendering to his feelings and finally acknowledging and experiencing them. He went through his period of "spiritual madness," but came out the other side with wide verandas of feelings and experiences available to him that previously had been drowned in his need to maintain a bland acquiescence to the world.

Jake's view of his god changed radically over the two years that we worked together. When we ended therapy, he was making a foray into Zen. He found the simultaneous attempt to control "negative" feelings like anger through meditation and the sharp whacks with bamboo that can accompany *satori* (enlightenment) to be a combination with both distinctly familiar and alien qualities to his view of the universe. While it could certainly be argued that Jake traded one spiritual system conflicted about anger, hatred, and aggression for another (see Chapter 5), it was inescapably true that in Zen he found much more peace than had ever been the case previously. He discarded the idea of hell.

Unfortunately, Jake's parents had not jettisoned their view of hell, and his turn from Christianity deeply troubled them. They became increasingly vehement about his having thrown away his salvation. However, unlike the experience of the dream, this was not devastating to him. As their increasingly desperate and shrill denunciations of his new path led to no changes in his journey, Jake's parents seemed to lose many of their own moorings. Ultimately they divorced, a scandalous event in their church. This raised an intriguing question for me, although I would never get the opportunity to know them. How deeply did their spirituality cover ambivalence toward each other, and did Jake's "defection" offer them freedom as well?

CLINICAL APPROACHES TO PARENTS AND GODS

Exploration and modification of parental identifications that have led to spiritual distress primarily happen through two mechanisms in psychotherapy. The first, and more important, is the experience of being related to by a nonjudgmental, accepting therapist. The experience of a relationship where the primary focus is understanding the client's world, and accepting that world without condemnation, provides a powerful healing force. It offers a significant challenge to the cosmic view that all one may be entitled to is judgment or punishment.

The second tool that the psychotherapist brings to work with clients in this particular area is, like the first, not specific to spirituality or particularly unusual. However, it is a skill that most of us do not attempt to pursue regarding the spiritual realm. This tool simply involves being spiritually attuned and clarifying with the client what identifications have influenced a spiritual position. This usually comes in multiple steps. First, the therapist must be able and willing to hear spiritual expressions in otherwise typical material from the client. Second, she or he must be willing to acknowledge that spiritual expressions are present. Third, the therapist must be able to connect how identifications with parents have influenced later relationships and also how these identifications have helped the client form a picture of her or his spiritual role in the universe. Such clarification can come about through work in the transference, discussed in a later chapter, or may be the result of pointing out to a client what seem to be spiritual conflicts in otherwise nonspiritually oriented discussions.

There is no simple, reductionistic formula here. Parents do not equal gods. They influence a client's perception of a god and in this way are useful to explore. However, Hillman's platonic argument that there is a mysterious element involved in the spiritual dimension of why a particular child ends up with particular parents is valuable to remember in this regard. Therefore, therapists working with a client's parental identifications can best understand these as forming something of a foundation on which experiences of spirituality are built, but not its entirety. Spirituality is influenced as much by mystery and the unknown as the known. One of the greatest mysteries to me seems mundane at first glance but becomes more profound the more time it is considered: how the pattern of spiritual belief began. Of course, one can trace a pattern, like Jane's or Jake's, over multiple generations of a family. But where and why did it begin? Was it sociological, economic, or religious in its very origins? Whenever I find myself attempting to reduce all spiritual dilemmas to the equation parents = gods, I think about this question. For me, it engenders a proper respect for the role of mystery in this equation.

CHAPTER FOUR

NARCISSUS AND PSYCHE

THE DEVELOPMENT OF IDENTITY AND ITS IMPACT ON SPIRITUALITY

Achieving and maintaining a functional and coherent identity has been proposed by recent psychoanalytic theorists, especially Kohut (1977), as being one of the primary, if not *the* primary, developmental tasks of the modern person. Narcissism is often equated with self-esteem in popular parlance; however, the term *narcissism*, as employed by Kohut, represents much more. It is fundamental to identity. Functional narcissism allows the individual to feel competent and confident and thus encourages ambition. It also allows for the regulation of anxiety and the psychic survival of injuries to one's sense of self. The ability to maintain a functional level of narcissism is an important and difficult task in the modern world. Spirituality plays an important part in the development of narcissism, and narcissistic development can also be one of the difficulties involved in a client's spiritual dilemmas.

THE DEVELOPMENT OF FUNCTIONAL NARCISSISM

Freud and his early adherents paid scant attention to the role of functional narcissism in development. Generally when it was mentioned, it was in a pejorative context, linking it with such serious psychiatric maladies as schizophrenia. Even the origin of the term in the myth of Narcissus implies pathology. (Narcissus became so enamored of gazing at his own reflection in a pool and wishing to be closer to the handsome man portrayed in it that he ultimately drowned.) Early psychoanalytic theory was much more concerned with the control of impulses than development of identity and self-regard. In the Victorian age, identity development seems to have been much more a foregone conclusion. Class, economic status, religion, career, and family defined the essence of identity. Reflecting this, early psychoanalytic theory was much less concerned with the development of identity. The cultural repression of sexual and aggressive urges and the hypocrisy that accompanied this repression were more important vectors in the development of psychological distress than is the case now. Freud's lifetime was the age of neuroses like conversion disorders.

In the second half of the twentieth century, and certainly in its closing years, psychotherapists have seen a dramatic decrease in the number of clients distressed by neurotic symptoms and a dramatic increase in the number of clients with disorders of the self (Kohut & Wolf, 1978). The primary difficulties that impel clients to seek psychotherapy currently have to do with the most fundamental elements of identity. Having lost many of the cornerstones on which personal identity was traditionally founded (e.g., church, social class, family), modern clients are often awash in a chaos of conflicting and contradictory roles and expectations (Kohut & Wolf, 1978; May, 1953; Menaker, 1989; Silverstein, 1993).

Kohut (1971, 1977) recognized this as the primary dilemma in the majority of his patients. He also offered a radically new conceptualization of the basis for this chaos. Instead of viewing the person as primarily the product of drives and their modulation, Kohut offered the proposition that basic identity is determined by narcissistic development. Later in his theorizing (1977, 1984), he challenged the traditional notion that aggressive and sexual drives are instinctual or biologically hardwired. Instead, he proposed both sets of drives to be products of the integration or disintegration of the self. For instance, one of the great debates in psychoanalytic theory has been whether aggression is an innate characteristic. Kohut argued that aggression largely, if not entirely, arises as a response to narcissistic injury.

Kohut (1977) identified three primary components or spheres of narcissistic development. The Gestalt of these he referred to as the self. These spheres or components of the self develop in response to a child's caregiving milieu and the responsiveness of caregivers (selfobjects) in meeting the child's narcissistic needs.

The three spheres of narcissistic development that Kohut identified as ultimately forming the self are the mirroring, twinship, and idealizing spheres. From the perspective of self psychology, narcissistic development is a process in which the internal and external are inseparably entwined (Wolf, 1988). The route that narcissistic development takes is determined largely by the interpersonal responsiveness of selfobjects. Current self psychology and interpersonal theory share much common ground, though not yet a common language (Bromberg, 1989).

For instance, in the development of the mirroring sphere, the child displays grandiosity, which invites a caregiver response. If caregivers view this behavior benignly and find it exciting or pleasing, they positively mirror this grandiosity, and, through subtle modulations of responsiveness, it ultimately develops into assertiveness, a sense of competence, and confidence. But if caregivers are threatened by the child's grandiosity and, instead of mirroring it, strive to suppress it, shame and a general view of the self as defective result.

Development in the idealizing sphere is predicated on the child's use of selfobjects to modulate anxiety and bolster self-esteem. Through idealization of caregivers, the child merges with the strength, competence, and confidence of those figures during moments of anxiety or threat. ("My dad can beat up your dad.") If caregivers are receptive to this idealization, the child ultimately internalizes the capacity to retrieve this experience of merger throughout development and can call on it or recreate it with other selfobjects at anxious moments throughout life. If the caregivers block such idealization (because, for instance, it elicits their shame), then the child may not have such comforting experiences to rely on when faced with threat, or the skills to engage a suitable selfobject.

Finally, Kohut identified a sphere of narcissistic development that he termed the *twinship sphere*. The child yearns to feel a connection to the rest of humanity. Essentially the child yearns to be one among a group sharing a common sense of identity and purpose. Optimally, caregivers respond to such yearnings with reassurance that the child does indeed share a commonality with other human beings. Such simple statements of reassurance as "Most people get scared sometimes" or "I think everyone has felt that at one time or another" are powerful twinship selfobject responses. The child feels connected to a larger group and therefore not alone in her or his anxiety. If caregivers, for whatever reason, cannot give such responses or can do so only intermittently, the child often develops a feeling of being "a stranger in a strange land." A common clinical manifestation of this is the client who feels constantly alienated from the rest of the world, who is not sure if the basic quality of her or his feelings and thoughts is shared by others. Such clients often feel that others around them were given secret knowledge regarding what is "normal," how they "should" feel, and so forth.

Although I have described these three selfobject needs and functions as if they could be separated, they are in fact inseparably linked, and any experience may meet multiple needs or result in diverse psychic injuries. Kohut's theory was radical in another way as well. Like most other psychoanalytic theory (with the important exceptions of Erikson's psychosocial model and Sullivanian interpersonal models), the examples I gave are predicated on developmental interactions between a child and primary caregivers, generally parents. However, self psychology also extends beyond concrete interpersonal interactions to include symbolic representations that can evoke parallel experiences to those interpersonal interactions. Each of the selfobject experiences described can be activated symbolically as well. For instance, a promotion at work provides a mirroring selfobject experience, even if not attached to a particular superior. Involvement in a cause that is seen as an attempt to better the world, a common experience for college students, can provide an idealizing selfobject experience. Similarly, being a member of a larger group or movement that involves shared goals, history, characteristics, or values can provide twinship selfobject experiences (Galatzer-Levy & Cohler, 1993).

Spiritual development can be affected by development in each of these areas. Often, difficulties with spiritual fulfillment can be traced to a difficulty in one of these three particular narcissistic spheres of development. This chapter explores some of the common difficulties at the interface of narcissistic development and spirituality that clients bring to the psychotherapist.

SPIRITUALITY AND NARCISSISM: THE PROBLEM OF SIN

The selfobject experience is predicated on one's seeing the self as valuable, competent, or similar in the eyes of one or more essential others (a term Galatzer-Levy & Cohler, 1993, propose to replace *selfobject*). These essential others can be present, fantasized, symbolically represented, or, more usual, in complex combinations of all three.

The spiritual practices and pursuits of life are particularly rich with selfobject experiences that have the potential to be either affirming or injurious. The potential for affirming mirroring selfobject experiences lies in acknowledgment for following the particular tenets of one's faith. This acknowledgment can emanate from two distinct sources: fellow adherents of that faith (which additionally supplies a twinship selfobject experience) and the object of the faith practice. However, to feel recognized as devout by the object of one's spiritual or religious practice not only provides a mirroring selfobject experience but allows one to idealize that object. Such an idealization permits merger with that object at times of distress, thus aiding in the management of anxiety ("There are no atheists in foxholes").

Difficulties can arise in the interface between narcissism and spirituality for a variety of reasons. One, narcissistically injurious identifications with parents, was described in the previous chapter. The psychic representation that a client maintains of a god is always influenced by human caregivers, especially parents. It has been my experience that the object of faith is fantasized in a human form. If a client's parents were narcissistically impoverished and unable to provide effective essential other functions, then that client's god is, to some extent, heir to those same qualities. However, there is another potential difficulty as well, which is culturally based and to a greater degree transcends parents. This difficulty is more generally confined to Western religions with a foundation in the Judeo-Christian tradition, because it is out of this tradition that the concept of sin arises.

The Judeo-Christian tradition emphasizes the superiority of God over people. This presents a narcissistic injury in and of itself. Beyond this, the Judeo-Christian outlook relies heavily on the notion of sin. How large a role sin plays in theology varies, with more conservative traditions emphasizing it more heavily. Nevertheless, sin is a feature of all Western religions. Psychotherapy, heir to the religious healing techniques of earlier ages, has had to struggle with the concept of sin, although it has always done so in a marginal way (cf. Menninger, 1973, and Szasz, 1961). Because it is religiously derived and has no scientific tangibility, the concept has rarely been discussed as having tangible psychological effects. However, the concept of sin does have deep and tangible effects on the identities of many clients.

Whether sin is a useful or valid religious concept is beyond the scope of this book; that the application of the concept to one's identity results in narcissistic injury has been demonstrated repeatedly to me in my practice. Castelnuovo-Tedesco (1991) offers the observation that individuals with physical defects or deformities often grow to view themselves as defective in toto, with the defect or deformity coming to define them to themselves. A similar phenomenon seems to occur spiritually around the issue of sin. The doctrine of innate or original sin encourages human beings to feel flawed and unworthy of love and acceptance. Clients often must come to terms with such a view of themselves as they develop or refine a spiritual perspective on their lives. An example of this process was Ted.

Ted was an educator in his early thirties when he began psychotherapy. He had consulted his parish priest about a number of issues related to career and relationships and had been referred to me. During our first session, Ted reported his major difficulty as his belief that "if people really knew what I'm like inside, they wouldn't like me." Our early sessions focused on relational concerns. His career, however, seemed on much the same shaky ground. He nurtured the belief that he was an incompetent teacher and although he had been repeatedly recognized for excellence, this "fact" would come out sooner or later. It was not too long into his therapy that a theme began to emerge that concerned Ted's essential view of himself as generally incompetent, defective, and "morally bad."

Ted was reared in a staunchly Lutheran midwestern family. He remembered vividly from his childhood the emphasis placed on human sinfulness and its offensiveness to God. He remembered church activities with ambivalence. He deeply enjoyed the ceremony of the church and its music but also felt guilty when he attended church services. Describing this during one session, he remarked, "I always felt stained."

Ted's parents were apparently thoroughly influenced by the notion of original sin. Humanity was innately flawed, Ted explained to me in a voice that sounded parental. He likened this innate flaw to the inspections that often occur on production lines and, smiling, he asserted, "We don't pass the inspector—kind of built-in imperfections." "Like a diamond?" I naively asked early on. "No, more like a weed in the garden," he retorted. Because of this innate flaw, Ted's parents apparently impressed on him the idea that pride was noxious to God and that pride in oneself necessarily precluded a correct relationship with God. Obviously, such parents were regularly narcissistically injurious; however, Ted did not feel treated in any more traumatic a way than any of the other children in the small town.

Within the first few months of his therapy, Ted announced in one session, "I think I'm angry with God." This announcement was something of a surprise because we had not been discussing God, and there had been no preamble to the announcement. He looked for a moment as if he thought the office floor might open and swallow him in flames. I encouraged him to go on. During that session Ted put the difficult issue of sin and narcissistic injury in the clearest light I had yet seen. He did this by posing three questions: Why did God allow sin into the world if it is indeed so noxious to him? If the answer is free will, then why must we constantly apologize for exercising it? How are we expected to feel loved if we are so defective in his sight and he has no tolerance for our loving ourselves?

Ted had highlighted the primary dilemma in his life; his career and relationships were paralyzed by this exact ambivalence. I pointed out to him my assessment that he was stuck in most aspects of his life in a quagmire of shame because of his sinful nature.

"What are you saying?" he bristled. "Are you saying I *should* be ashamed of myself?" Not stopping to allow me to answer, he demanded, "And just who the hell are you to judge me?" His eyes were fairly glowing with rage.

"Good question," I offered after some tense silence. "After all, I'm just like you."

He looked puzzled. He had clearly not expected that response.

"That's the dilemma for me when we talk about sin," I continued. "You, me—we're all in the same leaky boat, paddling with a crooked oar."

Ted smiled. "Yeah?"

"Well, if my boat is as leaky as yours and everybody else's is as well, who can claim to perfectly understand the ship designer's plan?"

Ted looked thoughtful and, for the first time I had witnessed it, at peace. For the rest of that session and several following it, he described his sense of being utterly alone. He was not acceptable to his god. No matter what he did, how well he tried to live his life, he would never be worthy of his god's affection or acceptance. His spiritual practices resulted in no mirroring selfobject experiences. Further, because he was not acceptable to his god, he could not count on his prayers to be heard. He could not idealize his god and use him in moments of despair. Finally, although he intellectually understood that original sin is part and parcel of humanity (in a perverse way, a type of potential twinship affirmation), he did not experience that emotionally. Instead, he felt alone and desolate in his flawed humanity. His spiritual practices offered him no sense of connection to his fellow believers.

It took some years to integrate a workable compromise to the dilemma of sin into his life. Ultimately Ted straddled the view that sin is an important and viable force in the world and the simultaneous view that it is also a mystery, which humans cannot fully elucidate. Having resolved it in this way, he gradually grew comfortable with experiencing pride and could then tolerate others loving him. Although not necessarily theologically comprehensive or even profound to many people, this was an important issue to resolve for Ted. It has been an important issue for other clients as well.

IDEALIZATION AND DISAPPOINTMENT

Kohut's study of narcissistic development asserts that the capacity to idealize serves important formative needs. The ability to allow the self to merge with someone or something greater than it allows a sense of protection and empowerment. It offers the capacity to modulate anxiety during crises and provides for the sense that one need not always face the overwhelming, and often frightening, mysteries of life as a solitary and powerless creature. This is one of the many attractive and functional aspects of spiritual practice. It is also one of the areas in which clients are most vulnerable to narcissistic injury.

The obverse of idealization is disappointment and devaluation. Learning to tolerate disappointment is one of the most important tasks of life. However, to develop the capacity to withstand disappointment, one has to experience some success in idealization. Put simply, the objects of our idealization must come through for us on at least an intermittent basis to avoid an approach to life that puts us always on guard for defects in other people and ideas that might prove disappointing. The cynic is the quintessential yearner for someone or something to idealize but is terrified of the possibility of disappointment.

Clients often search for the idealizable in their spiritual practices and yearn for the all-powerful and perfect god. They are often disappointed, and this, it seems, is rarely addressed. For thousands of years, Judaism and Christianity have been struggling to explain the presence of evil in the world. If God is all powerful, then why would he allow evil and terrible deeds to be done—even, sometimes, in his name? One explanation proffered has been original sin. Another, springing from the rationalist tradition, is that evil per se does not actually exist.

Rather, the universe simply operates on principles that we have yet to comprehend fully; this is a cause-and-effect argument.

These arguments, however, do not address the fundamental dynamics of idealization and disappointment. People wish to idealize their gods and are generally encouraged to do so by the persons serving those gods as clergy. However, there is generally not adequate provision made for the inevitable disappointments that accompany idealization. Such disappointments, if not effectively addressed, can scuttle an individual's faith.

It seems no coincidence that the second half of the twentieth century has seen a dramatic decrease in the memberships of mainstream Christian denominations. The second world war confirmed the first as more than an aberration in an otherwise benign universe. Further, that war introduced the horrors of both the holocaust and the atomic bomb. As Kushner (1981) points out, these events, especially the holocaust, strained all conventional explanations for evil and thus left the Judeo-Christian God an object of disappointment.

Interestingly, the traditional religions remained relatively unchanged. The bitter disappointment that has accompanied many of the terrible events of the twentieth century has not been addressed by the mainstream, especially Judeo-Christian traditions, and as a result has led to devaluation and cynicism.

The next logical question concerns how best to go about addressing disappointment on a spiritual level. For the psychotherapist, the answer to this question has three components. First, hear the client's disappointment without attempting to explain it away. Second, explore what that disappointment means to the client and what its historical antecedents have been. These first two steps are generally useful in exploring moments of disappointment that the client may experience with the therapist as well (Josephs, 1995). Finally, aid the client in constructing a spiritual view that encompasses disappointment but still allows for idealization. Kushner (1981) offers a remarkable example of this third component in his own life. After struggling with the dilemmas of suffering and evil in the world in the context of the traditional Jewish conception of God as all good and all powerful, Kushner reached the conclusion that an explanation accounting for all the paradoxes was that God may be all good but not all powerful. He leaves room for idealization but also disappointment. Another example of this was Michelle.

Michelle was an attractive twenty-year-old who was referred by her parents for therapy. She had been married for two years and during that time had suffered three miscarriages. After the last, she became deeply depressed and withdrawn. Previously a dedicated churchgoer, she stopped attending all church activities. Her husband, the same age as she, was in his first job as a minister of music at the church she had previously attended. He was dumbfounded as to how he should address her depression. He was equally anxious regarding her withdrawal from church activities, primarily because he feared that it imperiled her soul but also because it raised difficult questions for him with the church administration.

During the first session, Michelle did little of the talking. Her parents and husband accompanied her, and they described the couple's happy marriage and attempts to have children. With palpable sadness, they also described the three miscarriages, each occurring fairly early in the pregnancy. The couple had apparently wanted children more than anything else. After each successive miscarriage, Michelle became increasingly distraught. The parents and the couple's friends attempted to comfort her, but it was useless. During this first session I asked how they had tried to comfort her. A number of sheepish responses came, ranging from reassurance that she would be able to have other children to "It's all a part of God's plan" and "God will never put more on you than you can bear." Throughout, Michelle sat lifeless, appearing thousands of miles away.

During our first few sessions, I attempted to engage Michelle in conversation about her life and the miscarriages. She was only minimally responsive. Her only clear declaration was that she did not want to be referred to a psychiatrist for medication. During these early weeks, I would meet alone with her for part of the session and then bring in her family, not only to keep a pulse on their emotional states but to monitor Michelle's safety and encourage them to listen when she felt like talking without feeling as if they needed to have all the answers to her dilemmas. I also attempted to prepare them for what I thought might be the coming storm.

In about our sixth session, Michelle took her usual seat in the chair opposite mine. She looked hopeless and painfully distant. I offered the usual invitations to tell me about what was happening. She was polite but remote. Then, purely on intuition, I found myself saying to her, "You must be very disappointed with God."

She stared at me briefly, her eyes momentarily filled with tears. With some hesitation, she then composed herself and asked, "Why should I be?"

Wondering if I had blundered in my intuition, I offered, "Well, I don't think you *should* be, only that it would certainly make sense if you are."

"I've got no right to question God," she said clearly. For the first time she seemed present with me.

"Why not?" I asked.

"Because that's not my right. God's plan is God's plan."

"Okay, but do you understand God's plan?"

Her eyes again filled with tears, and she blurted out a wounded, "No!" She continued, "I've tried to live my life as a Christian. I've prayed. I don't understand it!"

"It seems like it would be devastating not to understand God's plan right now," I offered.

Michelle cried. Toward the end of the hour, I invited her family into the session. They seemed relieved that she was crying. I told them simply that I thought we might be getting somewhere but did not divulge what Michelle and I had been discussing, afraid that it might be overwhelming to them and that they might unintentionally choke off her movement in this direction.

During the next session, Michelle seemed present and for the first time began talking. "I've been thinking about what you said last time— about being disappointed with God," she began, appearing to be concerned regarding whether I was willing to confirm that I had indeed said this. I nodded. "I think I am, but I'm scared of it."

"It's scary to be disappointed with God?" I responded.

She confirmed this and then offered her history regarding disappointment. She had grown up with a great deal of it. Her father had been an alcoholic during her early years, before he found religion. As is the case with many other alcoholic parents, he would make promises to Michelle while intoxicated that he promptly forgot when he sobered up. Initially she had counted on his promises but had gradually learned to discount them to minimize her disappointment. She had never really discussed the issue with him; when he was drinking, it did not hold much promise for accomplishing anything, and after he had stopped drinking, she was afraid that she might push him back into drinking with any confrontation. I offered the thought that she might be seeing God as being as incapable of tolerating her disappointment as she perceived her father to be.

Over the next several sessions, Michelle talked about reconciling her disappointment with her view of God. Ultimately she opted for a more rationalistic view of God's role in the world. Natural processes emanated from God but ultimately take on a life of their own, perhaps far from his benign intentions. There were medical reasons for her miscarriages that were not tied to God's essential goodness. There was space for idealization and disappointment.

Interestingly, as Michelle shared this newly won view with her family, they were supportive but confused. Why was this new? Had they not been telling her this all along? It took an entire session to let them ventilate their frustration that Michelle could not understand this when they had offered it. This session also offered the opportunity to propose to them the possibility that some of the most seemingly simple and straightforward ideas require personal experience to truly acquire as one's own.

CONNECTION

The final sphere of the self Kohut proposed was that sphere concerning identity as defined by connection to others. Twinship selfobject experiences are those moments of feeling connected to the rest of humanity or another group with shared or similar characteristics, values, or history. During such moments, one feels the self as one among many. There is literally strength and calmness in numbers. In a spiritual sense, one derives some satisfaction and strength from the idea that one is part of a larger cosmic scheme that ultimately makes sense.

One interesting aspect of this is the anthropomorphization of gods. Throughout history, gods have been conceptualized as having essentially human characteristics in appearance and in emotional constitution. Psyche apparently began as a beautiful human woman before she was transformed into a goddess. The Judeo-Christian god is similarly portrayed in the Old and New Testaments in anthropomorphic images. He is imbued with gender, emotions, even physical dimensions (e.g., a right arm at which Jesus sits). The Eastern religions like Buddhism maintain anthropomorphic images to connect followers to the realm of divinity. For instance, in Buddhism, one's spiritual meditative practice often includes meditating on images of the Buddha.

Although there have been theological arguments against seeing gods as an extension of humanity, these seem never to have taken hold, and for at least one important reason: they go against the grain of identity formation and cohesion. One important aspect of an anthropomorphic view of a god is that such a god is like the conceptualizer. In other words, to see a god as being like some type of super being, although resembling a human, is to experience one's self as connected to that god. It is a manifestation of twinship phenomena.

Clinically, it seems to be more ominous when a client cannot conceptualize her or his god, or for that matter any other spiritual being, as anything like the self. It is not uncommon to work with clients who experience themselves as totally alien to both humanity and any type of organizing force in the universe. Often such clients were reared by parents who experienced the world as chaotic and unpredictable and often had difficulties with their own identities. Clients reared in other unpredictable or chaotic situations (e.g., multiple foster homes, institutions) seem to experience this as well. Their spiritual systems often reflect an inability to feel a connected part of the whole. Not uncommonly, they attempt to live up to a composite and highly theoretical ideal that has been pieced together from disparate experiences with parents, churches, and other spiritual teaching bodies that have not emphasized the integration of human capabilities with these theoretical ideals. Such clients often feel chronically frustrated and disappointed with themselves that they cannot live up to these ideals and hold fervently to the notion that if they could, they would not feel as alienated as they generally do. However, as a result, they often strive to be superior to the common human experience, not having a sense of being connected to it, which thus maintains their alienation.

One of the currently popular catchphrases that is often applied to such clients is *codependence*. They often seem to put their own welfare as secondary to that of those around them. They try constantly to please and are highly attuned to any feedback from the environment that they are not succeeding in this. They are highly critical of themselves for any fault and expect superhuman performance in all areas. Guilt and shame are their frequent, if not invariable, companions. This obviously describes many clients that psychotherapists see regularly; however, it is interesting how often this set of characteristics is not suggestive to therapists that these clients might experience spiritual difficulties as well as relational ones.

When I work with such clients, I find it helpful to attempt to understand how alienated and alone they feel and aid them in developing a language for this. It is then often helpful to review their histories with an eye toward understanding with them the role that chaos played in that history. Often what follows logically from this is an exploration of the spiritual facade they constructed to attempt to make some sense of the chaos and alienation. All the while this is taking place, I continually offer guidance from one human being to another as to what can be reasonably expected of a human being. While I recognize this final aspect to be controversial, particularly for psychoanalytic practitioners who might believe it to be a violation of neutrality, it is crucial to aid clients in experiencing an empathic exploration of their strengths and limitations. Such an exploration ultimately opens vistas for ambition and limits superhuman expectations. This process can be seen in the case of Eric.

Eric was in his mid-twenties when he began psychotherapy in an effort to deal with issues related to what he described as codependence. He lived with his elderly parents and was employed at a small shop. Although very bright, Eric saw himself as incompetent and believed himself unable to survive without his parents. Both parents were retired, and the family lived on a relatively meager income.

Eric's parents were apparently intermittently devout Catholics. As he described them, they would "suddenly go on binges when we were there [at church] all the time." Then, for no reason that he could discern, they would cool in their interest toward the church. During his childhood, the family moved frequently, generally one step ahead of creditors. Although both parents worked, they seemed chronically unable to budget for predictable expenses. Initially Eric remembered his childhood as "rushed." He described both parents as "doing the best they could," but he also remembered them as generally uninterested in his activities or feelings. "They believed children are to be seen and not heard."

Eric completed high school but never considered college because he thought himself "too dumb." I shared my perception with him that this was a rather harsh self-assessment and that I thought he could be successful at college if this ever became an interest. This occurred early in therapy, perhaps the third or fourth session. He seemed surprised by my comment and asked what would make me think that he could be successful at college. I remarked that his vocabulary, style of thinking, and general fund of knowledge suggested this. He seemed sincerely surprised and acknowledged, "I've never really known how somebody would know that."

Eric had a number of friends. Initially he portrayed them as much kinder to him than he was to them. When I tried to inquire as to what this meant, he simply said, "They're just nicer people." A more specific definition was continually elusive. As time went on, a very different picture of his friends began to emerge. Without actually complaining, Eric was soon reporting that he spent relatively large amounts of money on his friends. As I pursued an understanding of this, it turned out that he essentially paid for everything that they did together, even though he could ill afford to do so. Initially, I conceptualized this as an identification with his parents' traditional approach to finances. I offered a remark about this, and he readily agreed.

Well into his therapy, perhaps the eighth month, this pattern seemed to worsen. I continued to offer comments that linked his use of money with friends to what he had learned from his parents about money. Finally, during one session, he tentatively commented to me that this line of thought made logical sense to him but struck no real emotional chord. He then stated, "I really don't remember learning anything from my parents about much of anything." It then occurred to me that I had been quite arrogant and had pursued a line of work with Eric that I typically argue against: believing that I could conceptualize what was happening with him and educating him through interpretations. He had allowed me to follow this fantasy for the same reason that he bought friends gifts. He thought that I was more valuable than he and that he had no right to challenge my view. His willingness to do so finally—although tentatively—was quite courageous. When I commented on this, he seemed pleased but also a little surprised. "I've never thought of myself as courageous."

With this new opening, we revisited his development and relationship with his parents. He described himself as always feeling alone as a youngster. He had few friends because the family moved so often. When he did make a friend, he was reportedly continually amazed at the types of relationships they had with their parents. He noted that "their moms and dads told them stuff." When I asked what kind of "stuff" he meant, he could not really articulate it, although he felt his friends' parents told them "about how life is." Gradually a picture emerged of chaos in his childhood. Ultimately he refined his description of his development as "rushed" to mean overwhelmingly chaotic. "It always seemed like there was too much going on, I never knew which way was up."

His sense of alienation and isolation permeated his life currently as well. He gradually began to talk about his buying things for current friends as a way to end some of this. He had nothing to offer other than gifts, and these kept them around. However, there was more to it.

When I gently challenged his perception of himself as having nothing to offer other than money, he replied, "Well, I don't believe that, but I'm supposed to give other people things anyway." Why? I asked. Eric then told me that this was the way God wanted him to live his life. We were ten months into his therapy, and this was the first mention of God as having any relation to him.

As Eric demonstrated to me all too vividly, because spirituality was not mentioned did not mean that it was not one of the most important issues in his life. Again, a door had opened, and I finally stumbled inside. Over the next several months, Eric detailed a rich and complex spiritual preoccupation with a god that had very definite rules as to how life must be lived. What guidance Eric had not gotten from his parents about being a human being came in abundance from his god. The dilemma was that Eric's god made some extraordinary demands. College resurfaced. He related that he had not attempted to go to college because he had not maintained a straight A average in high school. "God didn't want me to go to college, because I proved I couldn't do the work in high school," he asserted.

Perplexed, I asked, "Everyone who goes to college made straight A's in high school?"

"I guess," he shrugged.

"Now, if that was the case I never would have gone to college," I offered. "In fact, I don't think I always even maintained a B average," I added for emphasis.

"Really?" he asked with genuine surprise.

Eric then proceeded to tell me about the other rules he felt defined his humanity. His god expected generosity at all times, without resentment or "selfishness," which was defined in the broadest possible sense to mean any attention to his wants or even feelings. He was not to feel anger or any other "negative" emotions. He was "to give and never count the cost in all things."

Against this background, Eric began telling me about other instances of his giving to others. However, there was a subtle change in his manner, as if he was asking me what I thought about these various incidents. He began by telling me about incidents in which homeless people would approach him asking for change. Eric felt compelled to give everything he had at that time, even if, as happened on one occasion, he gave away his gas money. I would ask how it felt to give at those moments. His initial responses were invariably, "I don't know. I'm supposed to do that."

"And where's that written in stone?" I asked playfully but quite seriously.

"When you do for the least of these, my brethren, you do for me," he paraphrased.

Feeling caught up short, I retreated.

Then one session he came in and related that the previous night he had been accosted by a man who wanted money with the flimsiest of stories regarding an automotive breakdown. Eric gave him all the money he had, although he communicated to me that he did not believe the man's story.

"How did that feel?" I inquired.

"Like I'm supposed to do that," he said hesitantly.

"That's not a feeling," I pressed.

"I guess I didn't like it. I needed that money."

"Perhaps you resented it a little, or it irritated you," I pushed.

"I guess, but that's wrong. I'm supposed to give and not count the cost. Do unto the least of these . . ."

"That includes people who are scamming you or lying to you? Now where is it written that we're supposed to let others take advantage of us?" I asked, fully prepared to hear a source cited.

Instead, Eric was quiet. He looked thoughtful. Finally, after several moments, he said, "I know you're saying that there's a difference between giving to someone in need and giving to someone who's taking advantage of me. I also know that that's right, but I don't know how to do that."

I attempted to empathize with his sense of trying to do the right thing and offered, "You know, you are trying your best to live up to God's expectations. I wonder, though, if God is expecting you to be superhuman."

He acknowledged that he had never considered the possibility that his god's expectations might be extraordinary. Over the next months, we talked about the creation of his moral system out of those times when his parents had been devout in their church attendance. We also discussed his lack of real guidance in attempting to integrate his moral system with his feelings or with an understanding of how other human beings expect themselves to react to life's events. Essentially Eric had had no connection to other people through which to test out ideas about what can be reasonably expected of a human being. His attempts to follow the dictates of his highly demanding god offered him neither any human connection (because he was discounting much of his humanity, like his feelings) nor any real sense of moral accomplishment.

Eric and I worked together for over four years. Much of this work concerned specific interactions and his using me as an empathic self-object to gauge how I might react to these situations. Although there was much that could still have been done, our work ended when Eric enrolled in college. For both of us, it seemed a fitting place to stop.

CONCLUSION

The interface between narcissistic and identity development and spirituality is an important one, with each area reciprocally influencing the other. With many of the institutions and rituals that helped define the self gone or in transition, this is perhaps the most important developmental task for the modern person. We have often neglected to look at the tremendous role that spirituality plays in identity development. However, to truly be of the most assistance to the modern client, psychotherapists must become more cognizant of this relationship.

CHAPTER FIVE

LOVE AND HATRED

SPIRITUAL COROLLARIES OF AMBIVALENCE

O ne of the most difficult areas of emotional integration for most human beings concerns love and hatred. Often spiritual practices encourage the splitting of these two emotions, characterizing one as "good" and the other as "evil." However, both are necessary to satisfying relationships with one's self and those in one's interpersonal milieu. Further, in spiritual practices in which hatred is actively discouraged or condemned, the natural human experience of hatred can become a source of shame and therefore a perpetual narcissistic injury.

One of the challenges facing psychotherapists is to aid clients in integrating both love and hatred into a comprehensive worldview and developing an understanding that without one, the other is not fully possible (Goldberg, 1993). Working with the client to understand the role of love and hatred in her or his spiritual system is one of the key elements to success in spiritually attuned psychotherapy.

RELATIONSHIPS: A PRIMARY HUMAN AMBIVALENCE

Clients often express the conviction that the source of both the greatest satisfaction and greatest pain in life is relationships. One of the complaints cited most often by clients who consult psychotherapists concerns dissatisfaction in specific relationships, or in their interpersonal relationships generally. One immediate and imperative question presents itself from this: Why are relationships such a source of ambivalence? The answer is complex; however, one aspect of the answer must include the difficulty inherent in integrating love and hatred.

Early in life, we learn about the two key concepts of love and hatred. Love is generally presented as the ideal and hate as a source of fault and hindrance to relationships. One has only to be briefly in an environment with children and their parents interacting to see the origins of this phenomenon. Children are actively discouraged from being angry with parents, let alone hating them (Miller, 1981). However, it is impossible to avoid hatred in intimate relationships. The very first experiences with hatred evolve from interactions with parents.

Most novice clients, I have found, hold a rationalistic view of the world whereby everything should make rational sense. There should be clear, concise, and practical answers to life's dilemmas and difficulties. Relationships should be understandable along logical lines. From such a perspective, feelings are a constant source of frustration and confusion. Often one of the most difficult tasks in clinical practice is helping clients grapple with the idea that feelings follow a logic, though not a logic necessarily conforming to ordinary intellectual functioning. Put succinctly, feelings arise for specific and logical reasons, although these reasons are not always, or even generally, readily apparent to observation.

There are simple examples of the complex logic of emotions. For instance, one drops a hammer on one's foot. The visceral reaction is physical pain. The emotional reaction may be anger, or even rage, at the hammer, one's self, or someone else who may have had nothing to do with the hammer and may not even be in physical proximity. The physical pain follows a common logic. The emotional response follows a logical course as well, although this course is much more influenced by factors not readily observable or even identifiable, such as attribution of blame. For instance, it is entirely possible that after dropping a hammer on one's foot one might become angry with one's spouse, who asked that a loose board on the stairway be fixed. When the hammer is dropped, one begins to think, after the initial pain, "If only I didn't have to fix this damned board, I wouldn't have dropped the hammer on my foot." Anger begins to be channeled toward the spouse rather than the inanimate hammer, the self, or the task at hand. Equally likely is the possibility that one might drop a hammer on one's foot and experience anger at the self for being incompetent, inadequate, or clumsy. Although there is a logic that determines which feelings are experienced, this logic is highly idiosyncratic and difficult to grasp because it rests on so many intangibles that are difficult to observe—for example, history, perceptual idiosyncrasies, and unconscious motivations. Love and hatred are probably the most complex of all emotional reactions in this regard.

Melanie Klein and her followers have done the most to chart and describe the development of love and hatred in relationships (Grosskurth, 1986). They proposed that the origins of love and hatred arise in a baby's initial reactions to mother. Kleinians propose that these earliest experiences of love and hatred concern the breast and its functions in meeting the baby's needs. However, the symbolic nature of the breast can represent interactions with a host of primary caregivers who are responsible for a baby's well-being.

Following the Freudian tradition, Klein proposed that love and hatred are both outgrowths and elaborations of instinctual phenomena. The breast as the object of the hunger instinct was the primary area of Kleinian focus. Later theorists (e.g., Kernberg, 1976; Mahler, Pine, & Bergman, 1975; Sullivan, 1953a) emphasized the entire presence of the mother as a source of pleasure and frustration, and this has come to be the more accepted view. As Fine (1979) summarizes, "Both Mahler and Kernberg clarify the older idea that the earliest infantile experiences give rise to an organization of two sets of memory traces, based on the primordial quality of pleasurable-good-rewarding and painful-bad-punishing" (p. 310). However, for ease of example, mother as primary provider of physical sustenance will be discussed.

When mother feeds a hungry baby, a sense of physical satisfaction envelopes the baby, and gradually this sense of physical satisfaction comes to be associated with warm and tender affectionate feelings toward the feeding mother. If mother's timing is off in feeding the baby, however, then physical frustration arises for the baby, whose hunger is not satisfied, and he or she is left in discomfort. Out of this sense of physical discomfort arise anger, rage, and hatred of the depriving mother. Initially, the distinct experiences of love and need satisfaction and hatred and need frustration are completely split from each other. The baby experiences the mother as two separate entities: the good mother who feeds and the bad mother who frustrates. However, during the course of normative cognitive, sensory, and emotional development, the baby learns that the feeding mother and depriving mother are one creature. Although Sullivan (1953a, 1953b) points out that traces of splitting are discernible throughout life, splitting per se is optimally replaced by ambivalence at this time (the notable exception being individuals typically labeled borderline). The baby experiences love for mother for moments of accurate need satisfaction and pleasurable interaction and hatred for moments of frustration and pain.

This basic paradigm evolves across the life span. We tend to feel affectionate and loving feelings toward those who meet one or more of our needs. For others who threaten or actively frustrate our need satisfaction, we experience hatred. Across an individual lifetime, these two basic mechanisms are complicated by a wide variety of other factors. The very basic needs, like hunger, are joined by a complex variety of other needs, including companionship, subtler forms of empathy, sexual gratification, and narcissistic enhancement. To greater or lesser extents, we invite others in the environment to meet these needs. Often, to the extent that they can do so, we love them. To the extent that they fail at meeting these needs, they are hated. If this was all there was to it, there would probably be little difficulty in seeing the direct logic of these emotional responses. However, to this simple paradigm are added a variety of other factors, including perception and wish.

If love and hatred were always so simple as whether one is fed, there would be no difficulty in understanding them. Whether one is fed is observable, even quantifiable. However, early developmental interactions are much more complex and much less open to observation, verification, and quantification. They are much more vulnerable to perception, which is largely learned (Laing, 1969).

R. D. Laing (1969) highlighted the complex nature of family inter-actions. He pointed out that each and every interaction is multilayered and contains a variety of conscious and unconscious elements. These elements may be congruent or incongruent, or congruent in some ways and incongruent in others. For instance, a mother tells her son that she loves him. However, as she is saying this, her fists are clenched and she is frowning. The context of the interaction is that he has just knocked over her favorite vase in front of company after being told to be careful around it. As the boy hears his mother say that she loves him, he also sees her frown and notices the clenched fists. His ears register her as saying love, while his eyes register her anger. Additionally, the Gestalt of her response does not feel loving to him, and he is feeling guilt about having broken the vase. The complexity of such an interaction is over-whelming, although life is a continual series of such interactions. Laing proposed that it is in the earliest of these complex interactions that love and hatred are learned.

From these complicated interactions we develop a template through which to perceive the world. Laing (1969) describes the creation of this template:

> The internalization of a set of relations by each element of the set transforms the nature of the elements, their relations, and the set, into a group of a very special kind. This "family" set of relations may be mapped onto one's body, feelings, thoughts, imaginations, dreams, perceptions; it may become scenarios enveloping one's actions, and it may be mapped onto any aspect of the cosmos. (p. 18)

Stern (1985) proposes a similar developmental schema in his concep-tion of Representations of Interactions that have been Generalized (RIGs). Both conceptions suggest that through early interactions with family members or caregivers, we develop perceptual expectations of how feelings and relationships should be organized and that we tend to organize data from the environment to fit these expectations. The logic of some feelings thus becomes hazier. However, in addition to the possibility that the perceptual template created may not make sense to an outside observer (for instance, that after enough such interactions with his mother, the boy above might come to call her reaction "love"), it may be equally confusing to the self. Laing (1969) also describes this:

> The most common situation I encounter in families is when what I think is going on bears almost no resemblance to what anyone in the family experiences or thinks is happening, whether or not this coincides with common sense. Maybe no one knows what is happening. . . . We would know more of what is going on if we were not forbidden to do so, and forbidden to realize that we are forbidden to do so. (p. 77)

Why would we be forbidden to know what is going on and forbidden to know why we are forbidden? Part of the answer to this question has to do with the moral absolutism that is generally attached to love and hatred.

SPIRITUALITY, LOVE, AND HATRED

In no other area are love and hatred more complexly entwined and ill understood than in the area of spirituality. In my practice, many of the clients with whom I work experience deep conflicts related to feelings of love and hatred. Generally the source of these conflicts is a belief that they must love those they do not and must not hate those they do. Often, as therapy progresses, we discover the source of these contentions located within the template created by original family dynamics, which have been partially created and reinforced by cultural and spiritual teachings.

This aversion to anger and hatred is not confined to Western culture. Although many of the spiritual difficulties that distress clients are specifically products of Western spiritual practices, this particular dynamic is not. Although some Eastern spiritual systems, especially Buddhism, address the natural quality of anger and hatred, they ultimately see these as "negative" emotions that are to be mastered and will ultimately disappear (see, for instance, Hanh, 1991). The fear of hatred seems to be universal. This phobic reaction is partly the result of the fear of actions that can result from hatred and anger. Tracing the complete origin of this fear would go wide afield of the point, but it may be that spiritual practices emphasizing the fear of hatred grew out of attempts to ensure human survival. In any case, this fear seems to be deeply rooted in the human psyche, regardless of culture. For purposes of this chapter, the Judeo-Christian influence will be highlighted, but it seems to offer no more difficulty than any other spiritual tradition.

The Judeo-Christian Bible encourages the love of God in various ways over multiple applications. It also actively discourages feelings of animosity, doubt, disrespect, or hatred toward God. However, the god presented in this Bible is one who can actively frustrate the meeting of human needs. This god requires much: faith even in the face of adversity such as that faced by Job, the willingness to sacrifice an only son in the case of Abraham and Isaac, the willingness to turn from those who mistreat us without reprisal, and so forth. This god seems to have a rich and complex emotional life, which includes anger, even rage, and hatred. The logic of feelings would dictate that some anger, even rage and hatred, be a natural part of the experience of interacting with such a being.

Christianity, however, and, to a lesser extent, Judaism generally strive to mute or eradicate such feelings. This is obviously not true of all denominations and churches, but the message most commonly available through the mass media does not encourage the exploration of angry feelings toward the Judeo-Christian god. As a result of being told that such feelings will lead to eternal damnation (on the conservative extreme) or at least the anger of God, many people suppress feelings of anger and hatred.

Many parents, influenced by this tradition, but also exercising a natural aversion to being the object of another's anger, also seem to have some difficulty in tolerating a child's hatred and anger toward them. Rather than simply acknowledging such feelings as a natural and rich part of the human experience, parents often attempt to suppress them. The result is confusion about the appropriateness of natural, indeed unavoidable, feelings and the intensification of perceptual blocks to them (Laing, 1969, 1970; Miller, 1981).

Often when working with a client who is struggling with conflicts regarding love and hatred, I attempt to label and differentiate those feelings. Almost without exception, the response to the word *hate* or *hatred* is a variation of, "Oh no, I don't hate anyone. That would be wrong." As we begin to explore the origins of this denial, clients often begin quoting the Bible to me. The most oft-quoted phrase in this regard is Jesus' admonition to "love your neighbor as yourself" (Matthew 22:39, Revised Standard Version).

When I ask the client what this particular phrase means, the response typically emphasizes caring about other people more than or prior to caring about the self. Pointing out that the phrase seems to me to equate the love of self with the love of neighbor, a look of puzzlement or consternation often crosses the client's face. It is interesting how often the admonition to love the self is denied (Lerner, 1996). When I point out that one interpretation of this phrase suggests that to love others one must have a respect and love for one's self, many clients react with some suspicion. These tend to be clients who have great difficulty in accepting the possibility that they have a right to think of themselves at all, let alone in loving and affectionate terms. This represents a very basic difficulty in narcissistic development.

For clients who do not find this idea so alien as to be immediately suspect, their reaction initially is to accept the logic of what I am proposing but to wonder about the point of it all. This opens the door for exploration with them of the possibility that loving and respecting one's self can mean being empathically attuned to the complete variety of one's affective experiences, including anger, hatred, and their variations. The process of discovering and creating one's affective life in response to cherished persons, including parents, siblings, or a spouse, can be difficult and threatening. For many people, however, the process of discovering and creating affective responses in the spiritual realm is even more so. Many clients can ultimately acknowledge that being angry with or hating a parent is painful but survivable. However, when they begin to contemplate anger with or hatred of their god, they become frightened of the long-term consequences. They often wonder aloud if such feelings will result in their being damned. Obviously there is no definitive answer to this and certainly not one that a therapist can offer. There is, though, a way to ponder such questions with a client.

I have often found it helpful to ask clients simply, "Why would God damn you for being angry?" Their response generally vaguely references the Bible but with no other explanation. We then begin to talk about the picture of God that would be characterized by an inability to tolerate anger or hatred. Ultimately this often leads to exploration of a god who is very much like the client's parents. At times, though, it also leads to a deeper understanding of the client's faith and a deeper conviction in that faith.

One of the memorable experiences from my own life was in studying theology as an undergraduate. I went to a small liberal arts college that emphasized the importance of asking questions and challenging dogma. Having that particular tint to my personality anyway, I reveled in the opportunity to pose difficult, and what I then considered blasphemous, questions in theology classes. Surprisingly, one of the consistent responses I received to such questions and challenges was encouragement. My theology professors were wise enough to respond to the challenges of a provocative young man with some understanding that they were an attempt to seek a real conviction about spirituality. They did this by pointing out the possibility that God is a being who desires intimacy. Because we do not hate those who do not hold a particularly important place in our lives, love and hatred are part of intimate relationships.

Such encouragement freed me to search various spiritual paths in my life. I ultimately decided to give up pursuit of the ministry as a profession and instead learn the craft of psychotherapy. As the years have gone by, I have become increasingly critical of Christianity as it is practiced in many parts of this country. However, I no longer fear the possibility that this will enrage my god and result in my damnation.

While this may be a threatening idea to some religious teachers (that if damnation is removed from the equation, people may turn away from a specific religion), it is extremely freeing to clients. As long as the primary motivation for holding particular spiritual beliefs lies in a fear of the negative consequences of not doing so, people will hold to those beliefs, even in the face of severe and significant damage to themselves. I have often heard clients relate that the ability to be angry with, to question, and ultimately to hate their god has opened a variety of experiences to them that allow a sense of more true spiritual intimacy with themselves and their god.

LOVE AND HATRED IN THE THERAPEUTIC RELATIONSHIP

As a clinician works with a client to aid that client in discovering and creating a range of affective responses, which include love and hatred, it can be reasonably predicted that these responses will become part of the therapeutic relationship. It was an old psychoanalytic maxim that an analysis was not complete until the client experienced both love and hatred toward the analyst. In psychotherapy, that is not necessarily the case. However, once areas related to intimacy such as love and hatred have been opened up for exploration, the client often becomes cognizant of the fact that he or she is in an intimate relationship with the therapist. Both love and hatred can then result.

For therapists, it is often one thing for a client to experience loving or hateful feelings toward someone else. We tend to be reasonably comfortable with this. However, it can be quite another for the client to experience those same types of feelings toward us. Depending on our own characterological makeup, some of us are more comfortable with being loved and some of us with being hated. However, to be optimally helpful, the therapist must work actively to master a level of comfort with both being loved and its variations and being hated and its variations. Just as therapists can come to represent parents and parental figures, they can come to represent important spiritual figures. Therefore, if a therapist believes that it is possible for a spiritual figure to react with equanimity and acceptance to a range of feelings, it is important that the therapist be able to do so. Therapists can come to represent a number of important figures in the client's past, present, and projected future; they must have some familiarity with their own feelings and the ability to deal with their own love and hatred to aid clients in doing so. One example of the process of helping a client to integrate love and hatred into his life was Bart.

Bart was referred to the clinic at which I worked by his primary care physician, who had been prescribing a variety of psychotropic medications for him for several years. Initially, these medications were antidepressants, but to these had been added anxiolytics and sedatives over the few months prior to the referral. I had an acquaintance with the physician, and although I was not surprised that he had prescribed antidepressants, I was surprised that he would have prescribed the other medications.

These were my first thoughts as I met Bart, a man in his late thirties with a thick moustache that accentuated what would grow to seem a perpetual scowl on his face. I offered my hand, which he ignored. I then motioned to a chair opposite mine and watched as he deliberately crossed the room to another and sat down. As is my custom, I asked how he wished to be addressed.

" 'Your highness' will be fine," he sneered.

I opened my mouth to follow up on this when he interrupted me.

"Look, let's get this straight at the outset. I don't want to be here. I'm only here because Dr. Jones sent me. I've got nothing to say to you. No offense, but all this psychiatry bullshit is for pansies. Real men handle their own problems, and they don't need some guy who has probably never done a day of real work in his life to help them."

Clearly he had meant to be offensive, and I was feeling offended. Additionally, I was feeling defensive and retreated to a somewhat canned response. "You're angry," I stammered.

"No shit, Sherlock," he shot back contemptuously. "How long did you go to school to learn that?"

It had been a long day and my capacity to be patient was low. Fatigue got the better of my response. "Quite a while."

"Well, good for you," he again sneered.

"So just why is it you and I are sitting here holding this unpleasant conversation?" I asked with clear exasperation. I vaguely realized that

Bart and I were already enacting a transference-countertransference drama, but I had difficulty extricating myself from it.

"Because Dr. Jones is tired of dealing with me and won't give me my drugs if I don't talk with somebody. Good enough for you?"

"Frankly, no," I responded. "That's not good enough for me. Whether or not you and Dr. Jones reach an accommodation about drugs has nothing to do with me, and to tell you the truth, at this point, I couldn't possibly care less." The drama was in full blush.

"So why did he send me here?" Bart demanded. There was, however, an almost imperceptible softening of his manner.

Still stinging but seeing this change, I proposed, "Maybe you had part of it when you said that Dr. Jones is tired of dealing with you."

Bart laughed and said, "I think I might like you—if I continue with this."

Recognizing that Bart had offered me a tentative olive branch, I asked him why Dr. Jones had started him on antidepressants originally.

He began slowly to tell me about a depression that had begun nearly five years before. He had had trouble sleeping, lost forty pounds, found himself wanting to cry frequently although he was loath to admit that he ever gave in to this desire, and had trouble concentrating on his job. He also found himself easily irritated and "angry with everyone" (some things had not changed, I thought to myself). In response to a question regarding what, if anything, had happened five years ago that might account for his depression, he seemed genuinely puzzled. As far as could be established in this first hour, a rather serious depression had begun five years before without warning or precipitant.

As our first session ended, I remember thinking to myself that although the last portion of the session had been uneventful, I would not be heartbroken if Bart did not return. He seemed equally non-committal, even though he made another appointment with the clinic secretary.

When the time for his appointment came the next week, I approached the clinic lobby with some trepidation. My heart fell as I opened the lobby door to see him sitting in a chair well away from everyone else in the waiting area. He seemed to exude a silent warning that kept others at a distance. I smiled and invited him back to my office. He walked well ahead of me down the long hall to my office and remained totally silent.

After closing the office door and settling into my chair, I looked toward Bart.

"Well," he demanded, "what is it today? Inkblots? Electrodes attached to my balls?" (Now there was an idea, I thought.) "Or just more talk?" he trailed off derisively.

"So, we're back to you don't want to be here but have to?" I asked.

"Yep, never left there."

"Okay, well let's save the inkblots and electrodes as options, but why don't we talk," I suggested.

He smiled wryly. He asked what I wanted to talk about, and I suggested that we begin five years ago. He informed me that he had already said all there was to say about that. He restated the symptomatology that had originally impelled him to see Dr. Jones. When I asked what time of year the depression had begun, he noted that it was in early winter, "about on the anniversary," he concluded.

"Anniversary?" I prodded.

"Yeah, the anniversary of my mother's death."

"Your mother died a year before your depression began?" I asked.

"No," he snorted. "I said the anniversary. That's a commemoration, not a time. She died about fifteen years ago."

"Can you tell me about your mother?"

"I *can*. Do I want to? Is that what you're asking?" he responded disdainfully.

"Okay," I grunted.

"Okay, but it's a waste of time. My mother was not a saint, but she was not a monster either. She had seven kids to raise with no help, and she did okay. She worked hard. She made sure we were well fed, clean, went to school, and church." For the first time, Bart's face clearly showed complex emotions. There were pain and loss, but also tenderness and affection. He went on to describe his mother as a continually harried woman whose husband, Bart's father, had left right after Bart's birth. She worked two jobs to keep the household afloat and delegated child care to the older siblings. She was often tired and impatient, he remembered, but she had a right to be. I asked if she seemed to be equally impatient with all her children, and he responded defensively that, on the whole, that had been the case. She was sometimes more ill tempered with him because he was the youngest and she "just didn't have time for it."

"You mean *you*, don't you?" I gently challenged.

"Whatever," he responded dismissively.

My lack of patience with Bart was more than just a response to his provocation. We were already beginning a familiar pattern for him. I did some calculation in my head and then confirmed that she had died when he was in his mid-twenties. I inquired as to the state of their relationship at the time of her death. He defensively blasted that he loved her. I then asked if he thought the onset of his depression might be related to her death.

"Ten years later?" he demanded.

I reminded him that he had linked the proximity of the onset of his depression with the anniversary of her death. He looked thoughtful— and sad.

"I wish she'd lived to see me buy the business," he offered. He referred to a store that he had purchased about six years before. "I wish she could have seen me become a success," he lamented.

"Would she have been proud of you?"

"She sure would have been *surprised*. She never really thought I'd amount to much of anything," he said with a smile. "In fact, I had always worked for my uncle until I bought the store. Just before she died, she made me promise that I would stay there until I retired. She knew I wanted my own business, but she thought I'd never make it." His tone remained unchanging as he related all this.

I contemplated the picture I thus far had of Bart's mother. He had not yet described anything approaching tenderness or empathy, and yet he genuinely applied the word *love* to her interactions with him. She had expected him to fail, perhaps attempted to sentence him to failing, at his dream of owning his own business. This was a confusing picture, at best.

Bart continued to appear faithfully for his appointments. He continued to bristle with hostility at times, although this decreased somewhat. Over a period of several weeks, we discussed little other than his relationship with his mother. He continued to describe her as a woman who had no tangible interest in or time for him but never once approached the possibility that their relationship was more complex than to be summed up completely with the word *loving*.

We had been meeting for approximately four months when I attempted to draw his attention to this. He was reluctant initially to give it more than a cursory thought. However, he gradually became somewhat curious about the possibility that this relationship was more complex than it originally seemed. An important moment came in one session when Bart acknowledged that, at times, it had seemed that he was "a pain in the ass" to his mother. He was confused by this, though, because she always defined her feelings verbally toward him as love.

Over the weeks following this acknowledgment, Bart also began to express a resentment he felt toward her, although he had been careful not to show it while growing up, he proposed. But never feeling that he pleased her, he was often frustrated and angry with her. For some period, he had apparently felt guilty about this, but when he reached latency, he began to feel keenly resentful of her treatment. Her continual contention that he would never make much of himself intensified these feelings. He recalled a fantasy he had around age eleven that she had died in an accident when she was late coming home one evening. After remembering this fantasy, he wondered aloud if this might have been in some measure a wish.

During this period, our moments of hostile interaction decreased, but they were still present in most sessions. I broached this during one hour and was met with a surprising response. Bart genuinely could not accept that there had been any hostility in any of our interactions. He seemed surprised that I might perceive anything he had done as critical, dismissive, or angry toward me. He reportedly perceived nothing I had done in this light. We reviewed some of these interactions in detail, and I pointed out comments that had seemed angry to me. On reflection, he could acknowledge that these could certainly seem disparaging, but said that he genuinely liked me and would not have meant to hurt me. He acknowledged at this point that others had made similar comments to him in the past. His only long-term romantic interest had ended with his fiancée telling him that she never felt loved by him. He looked guilty and proposed that he perhaps pushed others away at times. We began to look at the possibility that feelings were sometimes turned upside down in his family and that love and hatred might have been two of the feelings confused.

"Hate?" he asked with alarm. "Granted, it sounds like we had some problems, but I don't think anybody hated anybody else," he protested.

"*Hate* sounds like a strong word," I offered conciliatorily. "How else would you explain it?"

"I don't know, but *hate!* One of the things my mother did teach us was that it was wrong to hate."

"Agreed. It seems mostly, though, that she taught how not to acknowledge hate by calling it love."

"But that would mean that," he paused and looked terribly sad, "she hated me."

We were both silent for a long moment. Bart then asked, "Why would she have hated me?" It was an important, but perhaps unanswerable, question.

Although he remained reluctant to use the word *hate* and instead often substituted the word *angry*, Bart made remarkable gains over the next few weeks. He entered each new session with examples of interpersonal interactions offering ambiguity regarding emotional content. We processed many such interactions, differentiating anger from affection, love from hatred, hostility from warmth. He talked with one of his older siblings, who was shocked that Bart might be questioning their mother's kindness and love toward him. This sibling, however, offered an important new piece to the picture. Apparently, although it was consciously unknown to Bart, it was a commonly accepted family fact that Bart's father had left after Bart's birth because he felt smothered by the demands of such a large family. From this, Bart hypothesized that his mother might have blamed him for his father's desertion. "After all," he noted, "everything was okay until I came along." I expressed my doubts that everything had indeed been okay until Bart's birth but agreed that his hypothesis seemed plausible.

For several weeks Bart continued to work as hard as any other client I have seen in therapy. His symptoms decreased dramatically. Our relationship was less volatile. He expressed both appreciation and affection more easily, but he was also assertive in telling me when he felt frustrated or misunderstood. Dr. Jones called to thank and congratulate me on a miracle. Then it hit.

One afternoon, Bart arrived at his usual appointment time. I had grown accustomed to fetching him from the waiting room in the middle of a conversation with one of the receptionists or another waiting client. Today he was clearly alone. The older feeling of his being completely separate from everyone else in the environment returned. We traversed the hall to my office without the exchange of a word. He sat with a noticeable effort to turn his head from me. There was a palpable silence for what seemed forever. Then, his eyes ablaze with fury and hatred, he turned to me and spat, "You know, this has been bullshit!"

"*This* covers a lot. Do you want to be any more specific?" I queried.

"*Psycho*therapy," he hissed, with a definite accent on the first syllable.

He turned away again and there was another silent pause. Feeling dumbstruck, all I could think to say was, "Something has happened."

"Fuckin' A something has happened," he snorted.

Over the next few minutes I was able to piece together some of the events leading up to this interaction. Apparently Bart's older sibling had been concerned about the conversation they had had and called a conservative local minister. The minister had made a "healing call" on Bart, at the sibling's request, to help straighten out what seemed a dangerous spiritual tangle. Bart had been open with the minister and shared our months of therapy and some of the hypotheses we had arrived at. The minister was shocked and dismayed that Bart could believe his mother capable of anything but maternal warmth for him. He was even more horrified that Bart might have experienced anything but appreciative love and respect for her. The minister had quoted the commandment "Honor your father and your mother, that your days may be long in the land which the Lord your God gives you" (Exodus 20:12, Revised Standard Version). He continued by informing Bart that "the land which the Lord your God gives you" was heaven. He had impressed on Bart that hatred, especially toward someone who had sacrificed as much as his mother had, was an abomination. The minister had prayed with Bart and offered to pray for him so that his sinful hatred and anger did not drag him into "the pit." Bart was nearly in tears as he finished telling me about the "healing visit."

"That sounds like a very hurtful meeting," was all I could manage to say.

"It may have saved my soul. It's wrong to hate. It's wrong to be resentful," he began to list.

"Or it's human," I insisted forcefully.

"He [the minister] was trying to help me let go of my hate and resentment."

"No," I interjected. "He wants you to *pretend* that you don't feel those things." I was feeling angry now at this minister. "The world would be so much tidier if we didn't have human feelings. Haven't you already tried that?" I recognized that the minister had probably only given voice to some concerns already present for Bart but knew that this would provide the opportunity for Bart and me to struggle with them.

"He's a man of God," Bart indignantly protested.

"He's a man of *his* god," I responded, "certainly not mine and not necessarily yours."

"What do you mean?" he asked incredulously.

"I mean that whether or not your god is one who is frightened of the richness of human emotions is primarily up to you. There is a god in the Bible that seems to be frightened of our feelings, but there's also one who seems larger than that."

Bart's countenance grew calmer. We spent many weeks after this session wrestling with the thorny issues the conservative minister had raised. Bart read the Bible and was struck by how rich it is in human feeling. He was especially intrigued by the passages that portray God and Jesus as angry. He ultimately decided that a god who could create such feelings and tolerate their expression himself could tolerate their expression by human beings.

From its rocky beginning to our termination, Bart's therapy lasted about one year. Prior to our termination, he discontinued his medications. He experienced no significant recurrence of his depression. About a year after therapy ended, he called one day just to let me know that he was well and engaged to be married.

CONCLUSION

It seems to be both one of the blessings and one of the curses of humanity that we experience strong and conflicting emotions. Love and hatred are especially difficult to integrate because much of our culture seems to fear their integration. However, from the earliest interactions with mother they are there, and although they are perceptually deniable, in a practical psychological sense they are unavoidable. Further, to truly know more than a superficial love, there must be some capacity to tolerate hatred. Often spiritual practices and teachings are invoked to suppress feelings related to hatred. The result of such suppression, however, is certain psychological impairment and, to my mind, spiritual impairment. In the denial and avoidance of anger, hatred, and related feelings, one not only lessens the intimacy available with the self and other people, one lessens the intimacy available with one's god.

This chapter has looked at stark expressions of the denial and avoidance of hateful feelings. The next will look at more subtle ways that this goal is sought.

CHAPTER SIX

THE SEARCH FOR SECURITY IN MORAL ABSOLUTES

The recognition that a primary human motivation is the establish-
ment and maintenance of a sense of psychological security is one
of the enduring contributions of Harry Stack Sullivan (1953a), the
founder of the interpersonal school of psychotherapy. Sullivan also recognized that to obtain and keep a sense of security (although real security of any type is probably an unattainable goal), the individual uses a
number of intrapsychic and interpersonal defensive systems. As either
the threat of anxiety or the actual experience of anxiety intensifies, so
do the intensity and rigidity of these defensive systems. In contrast to
the classical Freudian emphasis on intrapsychic dynamics, Sullivan
(1965) described psychopathology as being based on the functionality,
rigidity, and intensity of these systems as evidenced in interpersonal
relationships. Kohut's interest in the development of the self mirrors
much of Sullivan's thought, although Kohut focuses less on the interpersonal dimensions of affect, especially anxiety management, and
more on the impact that such affects have on the integrity and cohesion of the self.

Both Kohut and Sullivan observed that as defenses intensify and
become increasingly rigid, there is a direct decrease in the individual's
capacity for empathy, which leads to a decrease in identity cohesion.

Both noted that the greater the anxiety, the less the tendency to be empathic with the self or with others. With increased anxiety also comes less coherence, stability, and congruence in identity.

Ours is an increasingly anxious world. This seems to be true not only in Western culture but across the globe. The traditional pillars of stability—extended family, occupational security, organized religion— are decreasing in both concrete presence and influence. There seem to have been a number of responses to this. One of the most important of these responses in the West, in terms of a consideration of spiritual functioning, has been a generalized decrease in empathy and a retreat to rigid positions of moral absolutism (Lasch, 1979). This movement toward absolutism has not been confined to traditional religion. Absolutism can be seen in some new age or other nontraditional religions such as scientology, and has been in evidence in the secular arena on both the political right and left (Lerner, 1996).

The retreat from anxiety to intractable dogma is not new; one has to look no further in history than Nazi Germany (or the reactionary theology of St. Augustine) to see it manifest. Despite this, there seem to be an increasing number of psychotherapy clients struggling to secure some internal sense of safety through adherence to externally originating systems of moral absolutism. The price paid for such tentative security is a lessening of the capacity for true empathy with themselves and others in their environments. This decreased empathy tends to block the discovery and creation of an ethical or moral code that is in accord with one's core values and life trajectory. It thus weakens general identity and blocks the acquisition of an ethical and moral perspective from the experience of immersion in differing worldviews and experiences.

It has always been one of the great challenges of psychotherapy to aid people in moving from positions of rigid and unempathic modes of interacting with themselves and the world to more flexible and empathic relatedness. A central task of the spiritually attuned psychotherapist is to help clients differentiate external moral or ethical systems from internal spiritual convictions arising from a genuine sense of self. This challenge seems all the more acute today.

EMPATHY AND MORAL DEVELOPMENT

Freud (1923) was deeply interested in the development of the internal systems and apparatus that govern the individual's interaction with the interpersonal environment. He postulated the superego to be the repository of ethical and moral standards. Composed of the conscience (proscriptions against specific feelings and behaviors) and the ego ideal (prescriptions for specific feelings and behaviors), the superego develops as a result of the internalization of parental admonitions, injunctions, and directives. Key to Freud's (1924) conception of the development of the superego is the oedipal conflict and its successful resolution. Through this conflictual period, the superego reaches maturity in the boy's recognition of his father as a rival capable of overwhelming retaliation. One key component of superego development is thus fear.

Freud's conceptualization of moral development has been challenged on a number of points, perhaps most heatedly in the past few decades on its incomplete formulation of moral development in girls and initial contention that women are morally less developed than men (Gilligan, 1983). Another criticism of this conceptualization concerns its reliance on fear of external retaliation as the primary motivation for moral development. Cognitive researchers (Kohlberg, 1984) have asserted that moral development is dependent on the acquisition of specific cognitive skills and functions. Researchers interested in female moral development have proposed that relational maintenance is the primary motivational element (Gilligan, 1983). Self psychology has offered perhaps the most basic criticism in the suggestion that classical psychoanalytic theory discounts the important role empathy plays in the development of moral behavior.

A significant body of research links the capacity to be empathic with the inhibition and regulation of aggression (Hoffman, 1979; Hogan, 1973). Both clinical and investigational research link deficiency in parental empathy with the physical abuse of children and suggest that increasing the capacity for empathy in such parents decreases physical abuse (Cornett, 1985; Letourneau, 1981). Feldmann and Johnson (1995) describe hostage negotiation as a process with multiple parallels to psychotherapy and describe a negotiator's capacity to respond empathically as having the effect of solidifying a hostage taker's sense of self and decreasing the likelihood of violence toward captives.

Galatzer-Levy and Cohler (1993) summarize a complex array of anthropological, sociological, and psychological research concerning moral development in children and conclude that empathy, especially the experience of being empathically responded to (or the converse), is an essential component of such development. Further, in a nod to Sullivan, they propose that "the very terms and processes of discourse about moral issues are socially determined, not universal" (p. 79). They note that there are developmental periods characterized by moral absolutism in the child in which events, feelings, and actions are viewed as all good or all bad. These periods are not based, however, on adult convention, even though they may appear to be. Moral development is always ultimately subjective: "children neither receive nor construct societal standards but reconstruct them with the help of adults—essential others—who engage the child with the moral issues so that he may reconstruct his moral culture within himself" (p 79). This argues against the possibility that morality can ever be anything but subjective. It also supports the notion that a universally applicable or absolute morality is developmentally impossible.

May (1953) proposed from an interpersonal perspective over forty years ago that true empathy is being replaced in our culture by a type of pseudoempathy. This pseudoempathy takes no real note of the complex feelings and motivations comprising the self and others, but instead simply attempts to gauge that which will be accepted by those surrounding one at any given moment. May suggested that the ultimate value often ascribed to the self consists in momentarily pleasing those in the environment. He sums this up well in his contention that "it is as though one had always to postpone his judgment until he looked at his audience. The person who is passive, to whom or for whom the act is done, has the power to make the act effective or ineffective, rather than the one who is doing it. Thus we tend to be *performers* in life rather than persons who live and act as selves" (p. 60). Miller (1981) echoes this observation from a more self psychologically oriented perspective: "We live in a culture that encourages us not to take our own suffering seriously, but rather to make light of it or even to laugh about it. What is more, this attitude is regarded as a virtue, and many people—of whom I used to be one—are proud of their lack of sensitivity toward their own fate" (p. xi).

The search for and embrace of moral absolutism seems to parallel the difference between empathy and this type of pseudoempathy designed for ready interpersonal acceptance and a tenuous sense of security. However, the key element of a coherent and cohesive moral code, true empathy, is absent.

THE EFFECT OF THE FEAR OF
ONE'S OWN HATRED ON MORALITY

Often, as a natural consequence of the split between love and hatred and the decreased capacity to tolerate the latter, people develop a keen awareness of any aspect of themselves that could be considered as having to do with hatred. Wishing to avoid this at all costs, they develop a code of conduct that emphasizes "goodness" above all else. Hatred is experienced as a defect. They seem to believe that the only way to overcome such a sense of defectiveness is through strict adherence to a legalistic code that prohibits certain thoughts, feelings, and behaviors and promotes others. The emphasis of life in such a situation becomes doing what is "good" or "right," especially in the eyes of other people, as if those eyes are the mirrors of God's soul.

The difficulty with such an approach is that it discounts the importance of what is true in what one feels. It denies authenticity. Such a stance is in direct contradiction of the true self, which Miller (1981) describes eloquently as the capacity of an individual to know "not only what he does not want but also what he wants and . . . to express this, irrespective of whether he will be loved or hated for it" (p. 33). The attempt to be righteous or all good lacks true empathy for the emotions that characterize humanity. It also requires the construction of a severe code of conduct, with which one is bound to fail in compliance. The shame that can follow not being able to live up to such stringent moral demands can be devastating and is based on the fear that others, perhaps as well as God, will find one unacceptable. Therefore, attempts to live up to an absolutist moral or ethical code are often exercises in frustration.

Attempts to avoid the *experience* of hatred (i.e., feeling it) are often quite stark and involve primitive defenses like splitting and denial. The preceding chapter dealt with such attempts. The fear of hatred can also lead to attempts to avoid the *acknowledgment* of hateful feelings. The intrapsychic operations and defenses involved in these efforts are much more subtle, less easy to detect, and generally more culturally and socially encouraged. They are nevertheless just as deceptive, to both the self and others in one's environment. They involve the development of a persona that touts love and altruism but ultimately hides hatred. Often these masking operations are based on sincere attempts to apply absolutist spiritual principles that are not authentic to the basic psychological and emotional constitution of the individual involved.

This chapter focuses on the defenses associated with the acknowledgment of hatred, toward both oneself and others. Such defenses can be seen in the search for moral absolutes across the spectrum of religious and political behavior. Two examples of this phenomena will be discussed: the secular pursuit of moral absolutism, embodied in such liberal notions as so-called political correctness, and the absolutism of the Christian right.

Although the label *political correctness* is a phrase of fairly recent origin, the concept of a secular search for moral goodness can be traced back through the history of liberalism (Schmitz, 1990). The liberalism of William Gladstone in nineteenth-century England is one example. In the United States, it has its strongest precursors in the 1960s in the struggles for civil rights and against the Vietnam War (Diggins, 1992). Like all other moral crusades, these began with focused goals. The goal of the first was to empower a group of people with rights that had traditionally been denied them. The second concerned a war that raised objections because of the specious intellectual reasoning that justified it and the social unfairness highlighted by its prosecution (McNamara, 1995).

In the past three decades, this liberal-as-moral tradition has broadened from its original focus on fairly circumscribed goals. With this broadening has come its confusion. Richardson (1990) proposes that liberalism is having great difficulty in describing its goals: "To the extent that liberalism has triumphed against feudalism, aristocracy, intolerance, and repression, it has lost the original historical opponents that served, by making concrete what it was that liberalism was *against*, to help infer what liberalism was *for*" (p. 1). He concludes that "on all fronts, liberalism can be seen as having unleashed social forces that undercut it" (p. 1).

As a response to this vagueness regarding its ultimate goals, modern liberalism seems to have embraced a broad goal indeed: that of ameliorating hatred, intolerance, and injustice. Although the last two might be achievable in some measure, they are weakened by the first, which is not only a human impossibility but an undesirable end in itself. The vehicle that has been used to attempt to achieve these goals has come to be called political correctness.

In its most extreme form, seen on liberal college campuses and in liberal organizations, the operational form that political correctness takes is a ban on discussion of ideas that might be offensive to a particular group of people. Often if someone has the temerity to discuss such an idea, he or she is shamed by the group. It is pointed out that this idea is motivated by racism, sexism, ageism, or any number of other -isms. The net effect of such a response is to label the motivation for the idea as hatred, which is never an acceptable emotion. Those of us in the liberal community often shy away from intellectual and emotional honesty to avoid seeming defective in the eyes of peers.

The stifling of honest acknowledgment of feelings and thoughts is dangerous to our culture in many ways. In a democracy, such suppression endangers the free flow of ideas that must be debated to maintain true democratic integrity. That, however, is much more the domain of sociologists or political scientists. For psychotherapists, the damaging effect of such suppression is the mystification to which it must ultimately lead.

Simultaneously attempting to envision oneself as a member of an open-minded and tolerant group while denying a range of feelings and the ideas that develop from those feelings as evil or defective is confusing. Like all other mystification, it demands that one become selective in perception. There are portions of the self that must be denied or inaccurately perceived to avoid loss of the identity derived from the group or censure from the group itself. These perceptual anomalies generalize to other facets of one's affective and cognitive life.

Psychotherapists themselves seem to be especially vulnerable to this type of mystification. I witnessed one example of this while supervising a group of psychotherapists at a social service agency. All were young, white, and politically attuned and saw themselves as liberal activists in addition to their identities as psychotherapists. During a clinical staffing, one of them presented the case of a young man who had requested mental health services from the agency. The presenting clinician described the client as a "black male." Immediately another clinician challenged him self-righteously: "You mean African American, don't you?" The presenting clinician blushed with embarrassment and acquiesced that this was indeed what he meant. Feeling especially brave that day, I asked why one term was preferable to the other. The first response was, "I'm sure he [the client] would prefer it." "Really," I proposed. "Has anyone asked him yet?" The presenting clinician responded that he had not. I then proposed that we were already beginning to decide for this client how he *should* want to be identified. A howl of protest arose. The negative effects of one hundred years of racism should be undone, the group maintained, by avoiding words that were disrespectful and outdated. After pointing out that disrespect must ultimately be for the client to define, I sat back to listen to the rest of the presentation.

The presenting clinician continued to describe what he felt to be the dilemma that initiated the staffing: he wished to place the client into one of his ongoing groups but was concerned that the experience would be injurious to the client because the group was otherwise all white. The other clinicians immediately supported this fear and related that his identity would be much better supported by placement in a group composed primarily of people of color.

"Why?" I asked with a little exasperation.

Because of inherent white racism, came a reply.

"Are you suggesting that all white people are invariably racist?" I questioned.

The answer to this, more tentative and quieter, was that this was not invariably the case (psychotherapists could, for instance, "outgrow" their racism) but that the majority of the general populace was racist.

"Is this invariably destructive?" I wondered aloud.

"Of course," came the indignant reply.

"So how are any of us to ever work past our hatred if we are never allowed to experience it?" I challenged. "I guess, more importantly, on what basis are we to decide what is best for a client and is that not injurious to the client in the long run?"

The room was quiet. This idea had elicited a knee-jerk response, but the clinicians were beginning to mull it over thoughtfully. Ultimately this interchange led to a fruitful discussion of the place of hatred and its unavoidability in human life. Individually, some of the clinicians later approached me to propose that the overly moral reaction that resulted from the discussion concerned a fear of acknowledging the vestiges of their own unresolved racism and hatred. We were then able to discuss the potential harm to ourselves and our clients inherent in attempting to avoid situations that might involve expressions of hatred, including depriving them of rich experiences to work through hatred and robbing them of the adult right to make choices because we, as psychotherapists, decide what is best for them.

Another example of the cost of avoiding the acknowledgment of hatred can be seen in Mario. Mario was an attractive gay man in his early twenties when he began psychotherapy. His primary complaint at the outset was that he could find dates, but none had become a long-term relationship. He acknowledged that potential partners often accused him of being "fake." Friends, too, had leveled this charge. He seemed sincerely baffled by this response from others as he described himself as "completely open, what you see is what you get."

During our initial sessions, I was struck by how difficult it was for Mario to acknowledge what he felt. He was never angry with anyone, never felt taken advantage of, never even experienced mild irritation or impatience. However, he was continually describing situations that would arouse some form of hate-related reaction: friends who borrowed money and never returned it, slights he received from coworkers, and rejections from sexual partners he had hoped might become romantic partners. When I would react to his description of these experiences, I would propose that such situations might elicit anger, rage, or even hatred. Mario would vehemently rebuff such suggestions. He did not feel such "antisocial" emotions.

Mario described himself as an atheist. His moral code, he proposed, was based on that which was "prosocial." Intellectually bright, he had a detailed conception of a world involving only affiliative and affirming feelings and behavior among and between persons. "Negative feelings and acts are antisocial," he declared. "There's no place for them."

Mario's parents had been devout Catholics who were deeply troubled by his homosexuality. When he came out to them at age nineteen, they rejected him immediately and completely. When he began therapy, he had not seen or communicated with them for over five years. Prior to this experience, Mario had also described himself as devout. His parents' rejection, however, was devastating and led him to reject the idea of a god. Instead, he had embraced a secular spirituality, based on the promotion of love and brotherhood. Much of our initial work focused on the terrible devastation he had experienced in this parental rejection, how it was replayed to a milder extent in the other relational rejections of his life, and how this might account for a part of his moral position. The first two propositions he accepted; the last was anathema to him.

After about three months of therapy, Mario came in one evening appearing troubled. He reported that he had done something "antisocial." He offered some specificity by asserting that he had exploited another person. I entreated him to explain further. He related that friends had asked him to accompany them to a male striptease act at a local bar. Although "morally repulsed" by the idea, he had accompanied them for fellowship. During the show, one of the models had struck him as particularly attractive. He had even placed money in the young man's G-string. Throughout the description of these activities, Mario blushed crimson. After leaving the show, he had returned home and masturbated. This, he said, was how he had exploited the model, because that young man had served as the focus of his masturbatory fantasy. A little confused by this description, I made the offhand comment that the model had aroused Mario sexually.

"No, he didn't," he emphatically asserted. "I don't lust after people I don't know. Real sexual arousal comes from real intimacy. You can't get that from a stripper."

I looked at him with what must have been a perplexed countenance.

"What?" he demanded.

"I'm confused," I offered.

"About what?" he snapped impatiently.

"Well, you described this man as attractive, you put money in his G-string, and you went home and masturbated thinking about him, but he did not sexually arouse you because that's possible only in a specific intimate context."

"So?" he again demanded, clearly not understanding my point.

"So it seems to me, and I could be quite wrong about this, that you are denying a feeling, which we have a great deal of evidence to support as existing, because that feeling does not match your moral ideal."

He looked thoughtful. This session ended soon after.

The next week Mario arrived appearing angry. He sat down heavily and shot a contemptuous glance in my direction. I sat, waiting for him to begin the session. There was a long silence, which he finally broke.

"I've been thinking about our last session—you know, what you said about how I felt about the stripper." There was a fire glowing in his eyes.

"Yes?" I said noncommittally.

"You had no right to say that to me. How dare you try to tell me how I feel? Don't you believe that I know more about how I feel than you do? So where do you get off telling me I wanted a stripper?"

I remember a specific fantasy that if Mario had been David Banner, he would now be changing into the Incredible Hulk and I would be in more than a little trouble.

"Seems like I angered you last time," I proposed.

"No, we've covered that one too. I don't get angry, even if I should." With the trailing off of the last word, his eyes changed. It was as if the fire that had been in them was extinguished by the tears that were now quite evident.

"Sad?" I asked.

Mario broke openly into tears. "I *am* angry," he moaned, "but it's wrong. I don't want to be angry with you. You're one of the few people in my life who hasn't given up on me. It's just so wrong."

I was struck by Mario's courage. It was not that he had completely split off feelings that violated his superhuman moral code; however, acknowledging them had been unthinkable previously. He was now doing the unthinkable. I commented on his courage and asserted quietly, "I don't know whether it's wrong or not—I don't think so—but I think those feelings are *real*."

His therapy moved quickly after this interchange. He explored a range of feelings, generally looking to me for confirmation that what he felt was human. Toward the end of his therapy, he related that friends had commented on a definite change in him. He apparently seemed "less fake" to them. He was also experiencing more success in dating. For the first time, he was being more selective regarding whom he saw more than once. Although he still struggled at times with feeling an emotion or attitude to be "antisocial," he could challenge this. Ambivalence was much more tolerable.

We terminated after six months. The man who left my office after his final session seemed much more able to tolerate his feelings and acknowledge them. His level of empathy was increased and, most important from my perspective, he had added true empathy toward himself and those around him to the "prosocial" qualities in his spiritual system.

MORAL ABSOLUTISM ON THE RELIGIOUS RIGHT

Like the moral absolutism seen on the secular left, that on the religious right has a long history. In the seventeenth century, it was Protestant conservatives who left England to settle in the New World. Although it is true that these people were fleeing the derision of their faith in England, it is equally true that their rejection of the other faiths present in England also accounted for their relocation (Robinson, 1991).

From the outset, the new settlers of America attempted to build a more conservative society, founded on biblical principles. They were against secular governance and the increasingly liberal view taken of the human spirit. Of specific concern were the roles being offered and taken up by women in the Old World. The New World settlements would have none of this, and women were especially restricted in their roles and lifestyles. Among a host of complex forces, the desire to restrict the roles and influence of women accounts for the tragedy of the witchcraft trials that engulfed Salem, Massachusetts, in the late seventeenth century (Robinson, 1991).

Modern conservative Protestant Christianity has remained remarkably close to these origins. It continues to bristle against secular governance, especially in the United States. It argues against the separation of church and state and promotes social roles in accordance with the interpretation of biblical principles, generally without inclusion of the word *interpretation*. The roles and prerogatives of women are still frequent targets of conservative ire. Abortion especially is the focus of much conservative religious protest. It violates two conservative norms: the taking of human life by other than the state in punishment for wrongdoing and the freedom of women from a traditional role as mothers. Perhaps as a response to the growing visibility of the secular left, conservative Protestantism and Catholicism have increased in both visibility and vehemence (Hunter, 1994).

Religious conservatives have widened the scope of their interests from the private moral behavior of the individual to the collective morality of the culture (Bennett, 1993). This presents two difficulties. The first is also applicable to the secular left and concerns the attempt to enforce conformity to moral principles derived by a source external to the individual self. The second, a corollary of the first, involves the mystification inherent in the confusion of morality and social role conformity. The first is again the province of sociologists and scholars concerned with social forces. The second is the province of psychotherapists.

One of the primary aspects of the mystification of conservative religious movements involves masking the role that hatred plays in life. Conservative religious leaders purport to teach a morality of love. However, one of the central elements of much of their teaching concerns hatred. Nonbelievers (defined as those not believing as they do) will be consigned to the eternal flames of hell. This is an image of incredible hatred, although the involvement of hatred in it is discounted and it is simply presented as a biblical truism. Other groups—homosexuals, feminists, humanists, communists—are vilified as "godless," and there is an active clamor for depriving them of basic social and human rights. This too is framed in the language of love: that they must be brought back into the loving Christian community and cleansed of their sins. However, one has only to watch a sermon delivered by a variety of conservative Protestant televangelists to see hatred as one or another of such groups is discussed.

Under criticism of the fact that there is much hatred involved in their biblical condemnations, conservative religious movements have created a more sophisticated form of mystification. This mystification is the rationalization that holds that it is the sinful act that is hated, not the person committing the act ("Hate the sin, love the sinner"). In this way, the acknowledgment of hatred toward another person can be avoided, even as the experience of hating that person blossoms.

Clients who have been influenced by this tradition often bring a great deal of confusion to psychotherapy regarding love and hatred. In the more extreme, this involves the inability to experience hatred consciously, as was presented in the previous chapter. More often, however, such clients are deeply conflicted about the acknowledgment of hatred. They feel it, and indeed have been encouraged to feel it selectively, but they have severe difficulties acknowledging its existence and influence. Such was the case with Jill.

Jill was a woman in her early thirties, with a quiet manner and a charming smile. She dressed simply and conservatively, but her overall appearance was dignified and attractive. She called the clinic at which I worked requesting to see a therapist for help with depression and anxiety, but she specifically wanted one who would respect her "Christian values." Her case was assigned to me.

After introducing herself, Jill sat down across from me. Her posture was erect, and her hands were folded neatly in her lap. She immediately asked, "Are you a Christian, Carlton?"

"What makes you ask?" I inquired.

"I want someone who will work with me in a Christian way. I believe that God can solve all problems, but that he sometimes uses other people for this," she said matter-of-factly.

"Does he only use Christians to help with this?" I then asked.

She smiled. "I guess you're not going to tell me if you're a Christian."

I smiled and shook my head.

Although I had expected this reply to end the session then, Jill began telling me of her symptomatology. She had become increasingly depressed over the past several months. She was not sleeping well and was irritable, especially toward her husband of eight years and her two young children. "They haven't done anything wrong," she lamented. She had approached her minister several weeks before regarding her difficulties. He had consoled her, prayed with her, and entreated her not to allow Satan a foothold by giving in to her anger. He encouraged her to find solace in the roles of wife and mother. Although she did not say so, I sensed that Jill had left the session with her minister feeling ashamed.

The first few sessions passed with Jill's describing various historical and current aspects of her life. Her childhood had been happy and full of the church. Her parents were devoted to their conservative Protestant denomination. There was much talk of Satan in her home, and she was denied various developmental experiences, like movies and school dances, to avoid the temptations involved. She was not allowed to date until she was eighteen, and her husband was the only man she had dated. He was a member of the same church, and both Jill's and her husband's parents saw the marriage as pure and "a match made by God."

When I attempted to discover whether Jill had been happy in the marriage, I often received polite but short responses that there was more to life than happiness. She was "happy doing God's work" or "fulfilling God's plan." This was the only happiness that she needed. Her children had not been planned, but contraception was banned by her church. She had hoped that she might work, especially in some church-related capacity, but the children had ended all hopes of this. Her husband, her family, and the leadership of her church continually reassured her that the greatest job she could do would be to rear her children to be "good Christians." During one session, she surprised me by labeling this reassurance "patronizing," because she had otherwise steered scrupulously clear of any descriptions that implied anger or resentment.

A theme soon began to emerge in Jill's descriptions of her life. She was not particularly happy in her marriage, and although she loved her children, she did not find the role of motherhood especially satisfying. However, she would never directly talk about her lack of fulfillment or the resentment that seemed just below the surface. Instead, she remained stubbornly committed to seeing her task in life as "what God has laid before me." About four months after we began working together, something remarkable occurred that changed this.

Jill's older son began the second grade soon after my first session with Jill. She mentioned in a couple of sessions that he did not seem happy about school but always dismissed it as the need to become accustomed to a new teacher. However, on one particular day, she arrived for her appointment appearing visibly distressed and agitated. Gone was her dignified, almost stately, demeanor. Instead, she seemed between panicked and enraged. I inquired as to what was happening, and she related that her son had been suspended from school for hitting another child. She was baffled. Did he not realize that violence was anathema to God? More important, did he not realize how embarrassing this would be for her? It would be definitive proof that she was failing in her most important role.

"Sounds like your son was angry," I noted.

Jill looked ashamed. "I taught him better than that."

"You taught him better than to be angry?" I asked for clarification.

"Yes," she muttered.

We talked for several minutes about my contention that it would be impossible to teach a child not to be angry because anger is an inextricable part of the human condition. In response, Jill maintained that anger is the basest part of humanity, implanted by the devil. Sensing that this was not a direction in which I would make much progress, I returned Jill to her sense of humiliation that she would be seen as a failed mother.

"Besides embarrassed, how do you feel about what your son has done?"

"What do you mean?" she asked distractedly.

"Well, you have given up a lot to be his mother, not the least of which is a career, so how does it feel that he has embarrassed you in this way?" The goal was to raise her awareness and capacity to acknowledge anger or resentment.

"I haven't given up anything," she hissed. "I have done God's work, and that's all that matters."

"So who are you angry with?" I wondered aloud.

"Nobody," she snapped.

"Really?" I offered incredulously.

"Myself," she shot back.

"How about your son?" I coaxed.

She stared blankly for a moment and then confirmed that she was indeed angry with her son. We spent the remainder of that session exploring both her anger and her shame that she felt something so out of keeping with her religious beliefs. We again discussed the possibility that anger is inseparable from the human condition and that shame in feeling and acknowledging it might be related to her depression.

Over the next few sessions, Jill gradually began to talk about her anger and resentment regarding a number of areas of her life. She did resent not having a job. She resented having no social contacts outside church acquaintances. She felt burdened with the entirety of rearing the children, with little substantive help from her husband. Most of all, she was not happy in her marriage. She had been unsure from the start but had grown increasingly dissatisfied with the union. Jill saw her husband as having much more freedom than she and resented this. Their sexual relationship was particularly unsatisfying; it seemed to consist primarily of the meeting of his needs with little or no attention paid to hers.

For many weeks we discussed all these areas. Jill seemed to be growing more comfortable in her ability to both recognize and talk about angry feelings. However, what I had naively not anticipated was that her growing capacity to be empathic with her hurt and angry feelings would upset the marital equilibrium. Initially, her husband began what Lerner (1985) terms "change-back" attempts that involved shaming Jill for her feelings. He would tell her that anger and resentment, especially toward him, were ungodly and unholy. When this strategy did not work, he forbade her to continue psychotherapy with "that secular therapist." He demanded that she see a "Christian counselor" recently arrived in town. With some hesitation, she agreed, but in an act of great assertiveness, she negotiated in exchange that her husband accompany her and that the focus of work with the new therapist be their marriage.

Although we terminated before I would have wished, much had happened in Jill's life. She was more comfortable acknowledging her anger and asserting herself based on it. Her depression was much improved, and she had identified her marriage and the roles she had accepted even though they were not authentic to her values as the real sources of difficulty needing attention. I never heard what became of the marriage counseling; however, whether it was successful or not, Jill had already given herself an important gift of permission to feel and acknowledge her anger and resentment.

CONCLUSION

One of the most difficult tasks of being human is the integration of multiple complex and sometimes contradictory feelings. One of the most complex and particularly troublesome feelings for most of us is hatred and its derivatives: anger, resentment, and the others. We are often supported in our reluctance to acknowledge these feelings as important and part of the basic human emotional constitution by moral systems that view such feelings as threatening.

In a world increasingly filled with complex choices and few corresponding certainties, it is understandable that we search for security in absolutes. There is no shortage of movements, groups, and systems, both religious and secular, that promulgate such absolutes. However, absolutes are not consistent with the ambivalence and elegant complexity inherent in the human condition.

It is one of the increasingly important tasks of psychotherapists to be able to assist clients on journeys that include recognizing, acknowledging, and embracing this elegant human complexity. To be optimally helpful to clients in this process, psychotherapists must have some awareness of their own internal emotional and cognitive landscape. It is to this landscape that we now move.

CHAPTER SEVEN

COUNTER-TRANSFERENCE AND THE THERAPIST'S VALUES IN SPIRITUALLY ATTUNED PSYCHOTHERAPY

One of the primary tasks for a psychotherapist of any persuasion, working with dilemmas in all areas of a client's life, is to understand the interface of the therapist's internal world with that of the client. This must include understanding one's personal value system and the effect that this internal world has on work with the client. Such an understanding aids the psychotherapist in a number of ways. First, it assists in more clearly formulating a hypothesis regarding the nature of a client's difficulties by differentiating what might be expectable for the therapist (which, while helpful, must not be the final word). It can also suggest shared experiences from the therapist's life, which can inform empathic contact. The capacity to understand one's internal functioning also aids in preventing the therapist's value system from dominating psychotherapy with a client. Hartmann (1960) referred to this quality as the therapist's understanding and managing her or his "health values."

There has been a great deal of study of countertransference phenomena, especially in the psychoanalytic tradition. However, because spirituality generally has been such a neglected topic in psychotherapy, the need to understand and monitor countertransference, including the therapist's health values, in this area has similarly been neglected. This neglect has led to conceptual vagaries and even concrete injuries to clients.

COUNTERTRANSFERENCE AND THE THERAPIST'S HEALTH VALUES

The concept of countertransference is almost as old as that of psychotherapy itself. From his early work with hypnosis, Freud recognized the tremendous influence that a therapist has on a patient. Although he recognized that resistance is a ubiquitous aspect of psychotherapy, he also wisely understood that resistance does not completely mitigate the influence of the therapist. Clients have a tendency to want love and acceptance. One way of obtaining these, learned early in life, is through compliance. This is perhaps more true today than it was in Freud's time. He especially recognized the potential for harm to patients when therapists or analysts enact their own unresolved neurotic difficulties at the expense of clients. Freud's breaks with both Rank and Ferenczi were due in part to his concern that their technical innovations were primarily the acting out of countertransference difficulties with patients (Ellenberger, 1970; Fine, 1979).

The desire to minimize the enactment of neurotic countertransference difficulties was also the impetus behind the contention that an aspiring psychoanalyst must undergo a personal psychoanalysis. Except in traditional psychoanalytic training programs, the requirement that future practitioners undergo some type of psychotherapeutic experience has generally been abandoned. The result has not been positive.

Traditional psychoanalytic theory generally conceptualized countertransference as involving unresolved neurotic conflicts that were essentially oedipal in nature. Just as transference phenomena were generally considered to be oedipally based, countertransference was similarly conceptualized. As psychoanalytic theory has broadened to include an interest in preoedipal development, the conceptualization of countertransference has similarly broadened.

Heinz Hartmann (1960) added a new dimension to the concept of countertransference. He argued that in addition to the therapist's neurotic difficulties, she or he brings to every therapeutic encounter a set of values that guide a conception of the treatment. Although he was less inclined to question the values that guide particular theoretical orientations, especially psychoanalysis, he did propose that the therapist approaches each patient with a set of values regarding what she or he believes to be "healthy" or "normal." He proposed that it is neither possible nor entirely desirable to do away with such values. They are an inherent part of the therapist's identity and aid in making decisions regarding courses of action about treatment. For the psychotherapist, these health values, hopefully informed by clinical experience and training and made more flexible by the therapist's own psychotherapy, provide a map of sorts. They aid the therapist in conceptualizing the material presented by the client and communicating this understanding back.

Hartmann also acknowledged that the therapist's health values, in addition to being helpful, can hinder effective psychotherapy. This occurs when the therapist's values regarding how human beings should function do not match the authentic nature of the client. The clearest example of this type of hindrance I have witnessed in my practice has been in work with homosexual men who had previously been in treatment with a psychotherapist or psychoanalyst who believed homosexuality to be pathological and attempted to extinguish its presence in the client. Such clients are typically deeply wounded and confused regarding their identities (Cornett, 1995; Isay, 1993).

Hartmann emphasized the importance of a therapist's having as much knowledge as possible about her or his health values so that they are not unconsciously imposed on clients. He highlighted the fine line that therapists must walk in this regard. It is impossible to be devoid of values concerning how life should be lived, and at times such values can be profitably brought into work with a particular client. However, the therapist must maintain values that are flexible enough to allow a client to pick a different path from the one that the therapist would travel.

SPIRITUAL HEALTH VALUES

Spirituality is really no different from any other area in terms of a therapist's health values. Psychotherapists approach spirituality with some basic prejudices, biases, and values regarding the nature of what is "healthy" spirituality. Even the contention that spirituality is not a legitimate area of psychotherapeutic interest is, at its base, a health value. These values are equally present in psychotherapists who refuse to hear a client's spiritual concerns or who understand these concerns as merely symbolic communications regarding parents, as in practitioners who label themselves "Christian counselors." While it may be easier to see specific health values in the latter than the former, such values are no less present in the former.

Health values are often, like most other areas of our functioning, not completely conscious and therefore not always governed by rational thought. This is as true for spiritual health values as for any other. Therefore, attempting to understand one's spiritual health values requires more than rational thought. For the psychotherapist, it requires some experience, preferably psychotherapeutic in nature, that offers access to the nonrational arena. The focus of this chapter will be on presenting some ways of thinking about countertransference in a spiritually attuned psychotherapy, including some potentially problematic spiritual health values. Countertransference related to spirituality, like countertransference in any other dimension of human functioning, is never completely resolved. However, it behooves all clinicians to attempt to understand this area of their functioning as much as possible and, when such countertransference presents tangible difficulties to clients, resolve it, however incompletely, with the assistance of their own therapist or analyst.

A PRIMARY VALUE TO BE CONSIDERED

When considering spirituality and the therapist's health values, it is important to look at several specific areas and for the therapist to search internally for an understanding of feelings and thoughts in these areas. A beginning would be to understand one's views and values on those dimensions of spirituality presented in Chapter 2. Considering how one views these dimensions generally and how they might play out in interaction with a client is a useful exercise. Perhaps even prior to this, though, one should develop an understanding of one's values regarding whether spirituality is itself worthy of exploration in the therapeutic encounter.

Many therapists seem to have great difficulty viewing spirituality as a legitimate focus of psychotherapy. Clinical experience suggests that if a therapist is opposed to exploring a particular area in psychotherapy, clients are generally quite obliging and will refrain from forcing the therapist to confront this area, even if it is one of immense importance to the client. I have heard psychotherapists offer a variety of reasons as to why they do not consider spirituality to be the domain of psychotherapeutic exploration. One reason is that spirituality is too deeply personal to be discussed—a response that generally astounds me. We encourage our clients to discuss other highly personal aspects of their lives: grief, love, money, sexuality, and others. Why would spirituality be any more personal? How could spirituality be too personal? It is one of the bedrock contentions of psychotherapy that there is nothing too personal to be discussed. Indeed, the process of psychotherapy is one of exploring those facets of another person that are deeply unique and idiosyncratic to her or him. Spirituality is no less an important facet of a client's unique identity.

I have also heard therapists suggest that they are not experts on spirituality and therefore do not feel competent to explore this area with patients. This response too misses the point. It is very doubtful that psychotherapists are experts in most of the areas they explore with clients. Sullivan (1954), I think rather naively, suggested that psychotherapists are experts on interpersonal relations. One has only to look at the personal lives of psychotherapists, plagued by the same interpersonal difficulties as the general populace, to see the fallacy in this belief. Sullivan notwithstanding, my observation in conducting supervision of psychotherapy is that one of the marks of a competent psychotherapist is the absence of the need to be an expert on all human difficulties. Therapists who embrace this position seem more inclined to tread the path with the client rather than giving convoluted directions. Such therapists also tend to use their personal idiosyncrasies, experiences, and human imperfections to generate a sense of empathy with clients.

Responses negating spirituality as a legitimate focus of psychotherapy may reflect a particular health value (e.g., only that which conforms to scientific principles is worthy of understanding) or may suggest difficulties for the therapist in her or his own spiritual development. As Freud's admonitions regarding countertransference would suggest, it is possible that we either do not see certain aspects or choose not to attend to certain aspects of our clients, based on our own needs and difficulties in a given area. For many therapists, spirituality would seem to be one of these areas.

Beneath all of the conscious reasons offered for avoiding the spiritual facets of clients' lives, there seems also to be a hazier discomfort for many therapists. It is at least a partial explanation of our avoidance of spirituality in clinical work that to do otherwise would bring us face to face with whatever is unresolved in our own spiritual lives. There is a great deal to spirituality that is simply and completely mysterious. Psychotherapists are no less prone than the general populace to be frightened by the mysterious. Many of us entered the practice of psychotherapy, in least in part, to understand the mysteries of our own lives. We searched for and often found concrete answers to these mysteries. For many of us, to face a mystery that has no certain answer is not in keeping with our natures.

It is also worth noting that the mysteries of spirituality can leave a psychotherapist narcissistically injured. Like Sullivan, the notion of expertise is important to many psychotherapists. Because ours is a craft that works with intangibles and is sometimes treated derisively by the larger culture as a result, we yearn for a sense of expertise and strive to describe answers that we have discovered rather than being content to have shed light on questions that have no definitive answers.

In supervising a psychotherapist who shows inadequate attention to a spiritual dilemma posed by a client, I have often found it helpful to explore these potential areas of countertransference: (1) the capacity to be comfortable with the unanswerable, (2) the need to be "expert," and (3) difficulties with the therapist's own spiritual development. Questions I ask include: What would you need to look at about your own spirituality if you explored this dilemma with the client? Is there a definitive answer to the question the client's dilemma poses? How comfortable would it be to discover that what the client is discussing has no definitive answer, that it is a mystery? How would it feel to know, and perhaps have to admit to the client, that you have no answer to this?

An example of the complexity of countertransference related to the devaluation of spirituality can be seen in a supervisory experience with Mark, a young therapist working on his first job at a social service agency.

Mark was in his mid-twenties when we began supervision together. He was bright and very committed to his clients. He had had very little exposure to psychoanalytic theory when we began but expressed an eagerness to develop knowledge in this area. As his primary supervision case, he selected a woman who was gravely ill. She had a debilitating disease with a progressive course, and although she was still generally healthy when her therapy began, she was beginning to show signs of moving into a life-threatening phase. Mark was initially reluctant, he related, to use this particular client for supervisory purposes. She did not show the type of psychopathology that he associated with psychoanalytic psychotherapy. However, he ultimately decided on this case because it was one in which he believed he would face the most serious challenges.

Mark described Susan as an attractive woman in her late forties, divorced and with a grown daughter. He was often struck by her keen sense of humor. She had been ill for several years but had enjoyed relatively good health. However, when she sought therapy at the clinic that employed Mark, her health was deteriorating. She was becoming depressed and feeling an increasing sense of isolation and desperation.

Mark came to his supervision session one day and related a joke that Susan had told him about how one obtains entrance to heaven. When I inquired what he made of this communication, he shrugged it off as unimportant and talked instead about his attempts to interest Susan in developing a support network. Toward the end of the hour, he related that Susan asked him if he believed in heaven. Attempting to maintain anonymity, he had not responded directly to the question but instead asked for her associations. He found none of them especially enlightening. I asked what he made of the combination of the joke and the question regarding his spiritual beliefs, and he again shrugged. When I proposed to him that Susan might want to talk about spiritual concerns, he looked at me quizzically.

Several weeks passed, and Mark seemed to be developing a helpful relationship with Susan. Generally an empathic person, he seemed to respond to most of the issues she raised with sensitivity, compassion, and interest. However, whenever she raised a spiritual concern, Mark attempted to interpret it as something else, effectively choking off detailed discussion of it. When I pointed this out to him, he minimized its importance.

During one session, Susan brought in a dream concerning her unsuccessful attempts to call a friend on the telephone. In the dream she attempted the call a number of times, but either she received a busy signal or the telephone rang several times as if no one was home. She felt hurt and confused in the dream. I asked Mark what he made of the dream and, with good insight, he linked it to the possibility that Susan was trying to reach him with a communication but was not succeeding. I asked what that communication might be, and he was genuinely puzzled. I pointed out to him that several times we had discussed the possibility that Susan was attempting to explore her spirituality with him. He looked at me with some consternation and asked: "You don't really think that's it, do you?"

"Why not?" I questioned.

"Because I wouldn't think you believed in all that mumbo-jumbo.

Aren't you the man who doesn't believe in codependence and multiple personalities? How can you get caught up in something so trendy as spirituality?" As his voice trailed off, there was a definite note of disapproval. He continued, "Didn't Freud think religion was a bunch of bullshit?"

"Well, I think Freud was certainly not a fan of organized religion," I responded, "but what does that have to do with this woman's spirituality?"

Again a look of frustration and confusion moved onto Mark's countenance. "You're serious," he pronounced, looking none too pleased.

"Yeah."

"What I want to learn is psychotherapy, not new age crap. If I wanted to learn about spirituality, I'd turn on Oprah." Ordinarily Mark was respectful, perhaps even deferential, to me. This last pronouncement had a contemptuous feel to it.

"What's that about?" I gently challenged. He asked what I meant, and I pointed out that his tone was, at best, hostile. He apologized, and I attempted to wave this off, suggesting that we were at a moment of learning something and that defensiveness was to be expected.

"Defensiveness?" He looked thoughtful for a moment.

I asked what his values about spirituality were.

"I don't know," he responded abruptly. "I've never thought about it much."

"I'll bet you have," I suggested.

Mark looked exquisitely uncomfortable and then stated, "I guess I don't believe that we need to be worrying about someone's spirituality. That seems the business of priests or rabbis, not therapists."

"How come?" I asked.

Mark related that he had no real answer. Our supervision session ended, and I invited him to consider this entire area further.

He returned the next week with notes from his latest session with Susan, during which she brought up a concern, again disguised as a joke, about getting into heaven. Mark courageously suggested that she seemed to be struggling with her spirituality, specifically whether she would be allowed into heaven. Mark reported that she looked immediately relieved and began talking about fears she had related to death and its aftermath. He also noted that he became almost unbearably anxious as she talked about this. His hands became moist and his mind began to race. He had to strain to maintain attention on what she was saying.

"What do you think that was about?" I inquired.

"I don't know," he responded nervously.

"Okay, let's go at this another way. What's your spirituality all about?"

He began earnestly, "I really don't know. It's all a mess. I don't know if there's a God. I doubt it, but I don't know. I don't know anything about heaven or hell. What's the point in talking about all that shit. Who knows about any of it?"

"None of us for sure," I attempted to respond reassuringly, "but this woman is facing the end of her life, and she has questions. You don't have to know the answers, but you can be helpful just by listening as she attempts to find her own answers. You never know, she might also help you figure out some of the shit you're stuck on."

Mark was not an easy sell on the idea that spirituality is an area of life worth understanding. His confusion regarding his own spirituality was a major part of this. As time went on, he attempted to be open to Susan's conflicts in this area. Many of our supervision sessions were spent processing his anxiety resulting from the questions she raised. As a part of this, we talked at length about Mark's spirituality. He had many of the same unanswerable questions as Susan. At times, I found myself anxious and wanting to be able to provide answers. At these times, I shared both my anxiety and my lack of definitive knowledge with Mark. After some experience of our doing this, he was able to share some of his frustration and uncertainty with Susan, without burdening her with his anxiety.

Ultimately spirituality came to be the defining conflict of Susan's therapy. Although never entirely comfortable discussing spiritual issues—and not yet sure of what his spirituality was all about—Mark nevertheless worked hard to help Susan come to some peace with her spiritual outlook. In the end, I think Mark was as grateful to her as she was to him.

ANOTHER FORM OF COUNTERTRANSFERENCE AFFECTING CLINICAL WORK

There seem to be two extremes to the continuum of countertransference in spiritually attuned clinical work. The first is the fear of exploring spirituality with clients, often motivated by a fear of the mysterious or unanswerable. The second is much more difficult to address but no less an impediment to sound clinical work. This countertransference difficulty involves the psychotherapist for whom there is no mystery in spirituality. This therapist has arrived at decisions, whether consciously or not, regarding spirituality and sees no room for any other truth. Such therapists, while touting the strength of their spiritual convictions, seem to be frightened of their fragility. Such rigid fragility is seen most often among so-called Christian counselors, although it is not limited exclusively to this group.

There is danger for both client and therapist in this situation. If spirituality is not addressed, as in the type of countertransference manifested by Mark, iatrogenic damage is done to the client. However, this damage is relatively slight and consists of the narcissistic injury of not being fully heard. This is an almost unavoidable injury in psychotherapy because no psychotherapist is so skilled at the craft that she or he attends perfectly to every nuance of the client's experience. However, the iatrogenic damage done by the rigid insistence that a client accept the therapist's spiritual worldview—creation of feelings of guilt, shame, and alienation from the self—can be much more significant. It is similar to the process of internalizing an external morality and claiming it as one's own, even though it does not match the authentic self.

The difficult part of this type of countertransference enactment is that it is often sought out by clients in a much more subtle way than generally occurs in psychotherapy. It is a truism, highlighted by the interpersonal approach to psychotherapy (see Searles, 1990), that transference and countertransference are inseparable. The interpersonal tradition in psychotherapy has been extremely helpful in pointing out that therapists are never able to stay external to the psychotherapeutic process.

Beginning with Sullivan, the interpersonal tradition described the therapist as a "participant observer" and therefore an intimate part of any psychotherapeutic encounter. As such, the therapist's affective and interpersonal reactions to a client provide important information about the client but, equally important, can never be isolated from the client's functioning, nor can the client's functioning be viewed as isolated from that of the therapist. In this way, the unfolding process of psychotherapy can be conceptualized as the product of the interaction of the client's values, history, and patterned responses with those of the therapist. Put another way, the client brings to the therapist a set of expectations, grounded in historical experiences and molded perceptually by those experiences, and invites the therapist to become a participant in a reenactment of those expectations. This could be broadly defined as transference. While the therapist invariably becomes a part of such a reenactment, the goal is to help the client consciously understand the origins of these patterns, which then offers some freedom to choose other interactional patterns (Winer, 1994).

The early Freudians suggested that it was possible to avoid countertransference expressions with clients. They saw countertransference reactions as an indication that the therapist had pathology in need of resolution. The interpersonal paradigm challenged this view and suggested that countertransference is not only unavoidable but ultimately helpful if properly managed. Increasingly this view is embraced by all psychoanalytically oriented models. The helpfulness of countertransference, however, is predicated on the therapist's capacity to see it as such and explore it with the client.

In the spiritual realm, this is an especially complex task. Therapists who hold rigid spiritual beliefs tend not to see those as open to question. For instance, if one holds oneself out to the public as a "Christian counselor," there is probably some resistance to viewing one's Christianity as a possible source of countertransference. Further, a client calling specifically to see a "Christian counselor" will not necessarily offer a potential transference enactment that could be helpfully explored.

There is some value offered by a therapist with a set spiritual worldview. A client who shares that worldview without internal conflict can find in such a therapist a twinship selfobject who strengthens her or his identity. During troubled periods, contact with such a therapist can provide a sense of being reconnected both to like-minded others and to one's god. For clients whose spirituality is not free of conflict, contact with such a therapist can be quite damaging.

Addressing this type of countertransference is necessarily complicated by the fact that it must be defined externally to the therapist, and therefore little motivation exists to address it. For clients, it may only be in therapeutic experiences subsequent to such a countertransferentially tinged treatment that the impact of it can be highlighted and processed. The exploration of this type of countertransference and the damage done by it was an integral part of my treatment of Betty.

Betty was thirty when she first came to my office complaining of generalized anxiety and nightmares. These symptoms had been present intermittently for several years but had intensified over the past eighteen months. In addition to her internal distress, these symptoms were beginning to interfere in her sexual relationship with her husband. Although troubled for much of their six-year marriage, their sex life had been steadily deteriorating over the past eighteen months. It had ultimately been at her husband's urging that Betty sought treatment.

In gathering history, I heard about a childhood characterized by abandonment and a good deal of physical and sexual abuse. Betty's father had been an alcoholic and left the family when she was three. Her mother apparently had a succession of male companions who lived with the family, which included a younger brother, off and on throughout her childhood. Two of her mother's boyfriends had been physically abusive to everyone in the family, and one had sexually abused Betty. Importantly, Betty never referred to it as abuse, rather, she had learned about "carnal love too early." Betty reportedly told her mother about this abuse but was told to "forget it," or she would be out on the street.

While gathering this history, I also learned that Betty had previously been in counseling with a fundamentalist minister-counselor. I was struck by her choice of this individual as a counselor because she had not belonged to his church and did not, at first appearance, seem particularly conservative in her religious views. She reported that her husband had urged her to see this person because he was "a good man—right with God." The husband's information seemed to have come from a friend's wife who had consulted him briefly and found the experience helpful. Betty herself had apparently been excited about seeing him because she wanted someone "with a Christian viewpoint." I asked when this counseling had taken place, and she related that it lasted about three months and ended two years before.

As is my general practice, I asked Betty what this counseling experience had been like for her. She looked visibly uncomfortable but responded that it had been "fine." In answer to my question of what had been helpful and what unhelpful about the experience, she fumbled for words and ultimately described the minister-counselor as "a good man" and claimed that the experience had been helpful, but she offered little beyond this. At that point, I dropped exploration of this previous counseling experience, believing that there were many more pressing concerns to be explored from her childhood.

For the first several weeks of therapy, we discussed the trauma of her childhood. The abandonment by her father had been devastating. She remembered him with idealized adoration and was certain that if he had stayed, none of the other terrible traumas of her childhood would have occurred. I was struck by her lack of a theory as to why he had left (her mother refused to discuss this with her) and wondered if she, like many other innocent abandoned children, held herself responsible.

During this initial period, we also discussed the sexual abuse and her unsuccessful attempts to enlist her mother's protection. She had done this first by revealing the sexual abuse to her mother. When told to "forget it," she began acting out in school, hoping to draw attention to her agony. This too failed and seemed to result only in punishment. Again, I was struck by her seeming inability to offer a theory regarding her mother's lack of protection, and again I suspected that she unfairly blamed herself. During one session, I shared my theory with her that she held herself responsible for both her father's abandonment and the sexual abuse she had endured.

"Of course," she said matter-of-factly. "That's already been established."

Taken completely off-guard I stammered, "Excuse me?"

"Yeah, my first therapy confirmed that I was responsible for all that." Her tone and facial expression remained matter-of-fact.

"How did you confirm your responsibility?" I asked, still somewhat taken aback.

"Sin," she offered noncommittally. "Punishment for our sinful natures comes in all forms. My punishment was my father's leaving and to be used carnally by my mother's boyfriend."

This session ended soon after this interchange. In the week that intervened before our next appointment, I found myself thinking a great deal about it. Because of the emotionally isolated way in which she described her responsibility for the trauma of her childhood, I wondered if I had come across a psychotic facet of her personality. Her overall personality integration suggested a borderline adaptation, not unusual given such a traumatic history, but this response seemed to go well beyond a typical borderline response.

During our next session, I reintroduced this topic by sharing that I had been surprised and confused by our previous discussion. She reported surprise that I would have been surprised. I asked if she had always understood sin to be at the base of her childhood trauma. No, she had not. The first therapy had made this clear to her. Her lack of emotional connection to what she was saying was still striking. I asked her to describe in more detail her first counseling experience.

She was dismissive at first, stating that the minister-counselor had helped her and that there was simply little else to it. I then asked her to describe how she and the previous counselor had come to the realization that sin, specifically her sin, was the cause of her suffering. Initially she was unsure how this came about. Eventually she reported that she thought it had been the result of her questioning why God had allowed these terrible things to happen to her. At first, the minister-counselor had apparently been able to hear and tolerate her disappointment and anger with her god. However, during one appointment, she had likened her feelings of abandonment to those Jesus must have felt on the cross when he questioned why God had abandoned him. Betty related that the minister-counselor had lashed out in a way she had not experienced from him previously. He demanded to know how she could compare her suffering to that of Christ. Did she think she was God? What right did she have to question God? Christ had died for the world's sins, including hers, but that did not mean that there would not be earthly trials to be endured as a result of that pervasive sin. Toward the end of this appointment, the former counselor suggested that they had done all that they could together and that prayer for forgiveness was what she needed more than anything else.

For some weeks after this final meeting, she had apparently been quite distraught. She cried a great deal and spent most of her days and nights thinking about what she had heard. After several weeks, however, it suddenly seemed to make sense. He had been right in his assertion that her sin accounted for her trauma. With this "realization" came peace, although she described this more as numbness than true peace—"kind of like when the dentist gives you Novocain." This numbness could be seen in her emotionless descriptions of her previous counseling and indeed of the trauma that was such an integral part of her life.

With the onset of this "peace" in her waking life came the onset of the most vivid of her nightmares. As she described them, her nightmares concerned abandonment, especially by God. Her father appeared in some, her husband in others, and the former counselor in still others. They did not appear together in any of the dreams. The theme of these nightmares was fairly consistent: Betty, either before or after death, was found unacceptable to an unseen figure she associated with God, and was banished. The nature of her defect was never entirely clear.

As Betty and I explored these dreams, we discovered a number of condensed symbolic images: the abandonment of her father, the abuse she had endured and her confusion about this, and her sense of being condemned and abandoned by men generally. Beyond these images was also her abandonment by her god. As we explored this aspect of the nightmares, her previous counseling experience presented itself as pivotal.

Several months into her therapy, as we discussed these fearful dreams, Betty linked them more and more to the previous counseling. She felt condemned by the former counselor. She felt betrayed by her husband who had suggested that she consult this particular man. The experience of her father's leaving her unprotected in the hellish trauma of her mother's home was reenacted. As she talked about these feelings and experiences, there gradually came to be emotion evident in her voice and posture. She was initially anxious, then sad, and then enraged. This reconnection to her emotional life was important and hard won. We were still left with questions, though.

The most basic question still concerned why her father had abandoned her. But before this question could be answered, it was necessary to explore the answer to this that had evolved in her prior counseling. Betty expressed the almost desperate hope that the previous counselor had been wrong, but she would not fully embrace this. We reconstructed this previous relationship and looked at several possibilities. The most probable of these was that the previous counselor had become embroiled in a transference-countertransference enactment, based on both his spiritual rigidity and Betty's provocative search for rejection and abandonment. This seemed to offer the most complete explanation for the previous injurious experience. It also laid bare the probable course that our relationship would take, which would require much effort to understand.

Betty's therapy lasted another eighteen months and focused on a variety of issues related to the trauma of her early life and the pull to reenact parts of it in the present. One of the most important aspects of her psychotherapy was understanding the dynamics of her previous counseling experience. Although the complexity of this experience could obviously never be fully understood because we had only Betty's perception to build on, it seems reasonable that part of what happened in it involved a damaging countertransference reaction by the counselor that arose from an interplay of factors related to the personality dynamics of both participants; however, it seems likely that an important dynamic in this regard was a rigidity in the counselor's spiritual worldview that made it vulnerable to threat and required that it be defended—in this instance, at Betty's expense.

CONCLUSION

Countertransference has a rich and complex history in psychotherapy. Once thought of as a sign of therapist immaturity, the concept seems to be evolving toward a more flexible, perhaps ambivalent construct. Countertransference is now generally considered to impart useful information regarding both participants in a psychotherapeutic relationship.

Hartmann's conception of countertransference as involving the therapist's value system is particularly important in the context of spiritual concerns. The more the therapist understands her or his values regarding spirituality and its role in human life, the less likely these values are to intrude negatively on work with clients.

Equally important to understanding one's spiritual values is the capacity to tolerate divergence from them by clients. Flexibility in one's spiritual system, the ability to allow some challenge, is crucial to effective clinical work in the spiritual dimension of human development. Indeed, flexibility is one of the key aspects of clinical technique, the focus of the next chapter.

CHAPTER EIGHT

SPIRITUALLY ATTUNED PSYCHOTHERAPEUTIC "TECHNIQUE"

P sychotherapy has often been conceptualized as an activity driven by technique. Since the advent of psychoanalysis, there have been literally thousands of books written on psychotherapeutic technique and tens of thousands of journal articles and professional papers on the topic. Freud wrote voluminously about the activities of the therapist or analyst and stressed technique (even though he seems not to have followed many of his own directives) as potentially the most important factor in treatment outcome. Subsequent psychoanalytic writers have similarly stressed the activities conducted by the therapist when describing psychotherapy. Outside the psychoanalytic tradition, this has been true of most other forms of therapy as well: behavioral, cognitive, strategic, family systems, Gestalt, and others.

One psychotherapeutic tradition has been a notable exception to this trend. This tradition has not stressed the psychotherapist as technician but instead focused on the person of the therapist and the relationship created between therapist and client. This tradition is the client- or person-centered approach, which began with the work of Carl Rogers (1942, 1951). Rogers offered a conceptualization of psychotherapy that was truly novel when first proposed and still is controversial. Instead of the therapist's doing something for or to a client,

138

Rogers argued that clients overcome whatever obstacles have impeded their development if a certain type of ambiance and relationship is created in therapy. The therapist obviously contributes to the creation of this ambiance and environment, so in a strict sense a technique is employed; however, Rogers (1957) deemphasized the traditional notion of psychotherapeutic technique and instead focused on what he termed "the necessary and sufficient conditions" of a therapeutic ambiance: two human beings in emotional contact, a client in a state of psychological incongruence, a therapist in a state of psychological congruence (i.e., the therapist is genuine), unconditional positive regard for the client by the therapist, an attempt by the therapist to understand the client empathically and communicate this understanding, and achievement of the communication of both empathy and unconditional positive regard. These necessary and sufficient conditions have served as a starting point for subsequent discussions of person-centered "technique" (Watson, 1984; Bozarth, 1990).

Person-centered therapists emphasize the therapeutic relationship as very much a reciprocal endeavor, potentially beneficial to both parties. This is another way that the person-centered tradition has differed from more psychoanalytically oriented conceptions of treatment. Exceptions to this final statement can be found within the interpersonal tradition of psychoanalysis (e.g., Searles, 1990) and the existential dynamic tradition, including Laing (1967), who describes psychotherapy as the *"obstinate attempt of two people to recover the wholeness of being human through the relationship between them"* (p. 53).

THE PERSON OF THE PSYCHOTHERAPIST AND SPIRITUAL GROWTH

I emphasize the person-centered tradition in its conception of "technique" because for the psychotherapist who works with clients regarding spiritual issues, who that person *is* and the views he or she holds are much more important than what the person *does*. Elsewhere (Cornett, 1993, 1995), I have described a number of factors that serve to facilitate clinical work. These factors are, in some ways, Rogers's necessary and sufficient conditions recast in psychodynamic terms and conceptualized dynamically: the modification of anonymity to include self-disclosures by the therapist that support the client's identity; conceptualizing neutrality as an outgrowth of curiosity; respect, which emphasizes the therapist's honesty; courtesy, emphasizing the process of socializing a client to the experience of psychotherapy; and sensitivity, which emphasizes understanding the client as a part of a cultural or subcultural context.

For the psychotherapist working with spiritual issues, these qualities are important. Perhaps more important are additional qualities and activities that specifically address the complex nature of spiritual development and its expression in psychotherapy: curiosity, a comfort with mystery, containment, empathy, amplification, and the willingness to look at one's own internal world. Each of these additional qualities will be discussed below. It is important to emphasize that I am suggesting that the technique of spiritually attuned psychotherapy is primarily attitudinal and is therefore applicable to a wide range of theoretical models. However, it will be cast in more psychodynamic terms here because of the limitations of my particular training and experience.

NEUTRALITY AS CURIOSITY

The traditional psychoanalytic literature emphasizes the importance of the therapist or analyst's not losing an objective distance from the client by siding with one part of her or his psychic functioning over another. Put another way, one popular conception of neutrality is that it is the therapist's refusal to support, for instance, the client's superego at the expense of the ego (see Schafer, 1983). This objective distance purportedly prevents a number of potential difficulties, including the client's experiencing a sense of condemnation. The difficulty with this conception of neutrality is that with disorders of the self (i.e., disorders of fundamental identity), it often does not feel very neutral to the client. Instead, clients often feel judged by the silence and "objectivity" that generally characterize this traditional conception of neutrality.

A more helpful conception of therapeutic neutrality has best been articulated by Isay (1993) as an active, nonjudgmental curiosity. It is an approach to clients that emphasizes an interest in understanding. The experience of the therapist as curious is more helpful than that of the therapist as objective. Beyond this, however, this type of curiosity is powerfully ameliorative.

Curiosity could legitimately be conceptualized as the opposite of condemnation. The curious therapist offers the client a model for emulation of curiosity about the self. Many of the clients who are seen in current clinical practice are contemptuous and condemning of themselves and others, as well as manifesting a decreased level of curiosity. This seems to be both the result of denying aspects of themselves, paradoxically their hatred, and a response to an increasingly unempathic and injurious culture (Lasch, 1979; Miller, 1981).

In the area of spiritual development, it is especially crucial that the therapist approach clients with consistent and earnest curiosity. The very nature of spirituality makes it a difficult subject for many clients to broach, and an earnest curiosity on the part of the therapist eases the client's concerns that discussing this topic will inevitably lead to negative consequences. A curious therapist can overcome our culture's admonitions to avoid discussion of religion, spirituality, and politics. Such a therapist also fosters a tendency in the client to approach herself or himself with curiosity. Approaching the self with curiosity increases the likelihood of approaching others similarly. Thus, the client's likelihood of responding to others with condemnation or contempt is decreased.

One general prerequisite to curiosity, especially in the therapeutic relationship, is flexibility. Rigidity and dogmatism work actively against curiosity and tend to encourage whatever level of these qualities are already present in the client. Because it is often dogmatism that has given rise to a particular client's spiritual dilemmas, an experience with a flexible, nondogmatic therapist can be helpful, even if little else about the experience is.

Consistent curiosity by the therapist toward the client respects the inherent mysteries of spirituality. A therapist is best served by curiosity because there are no definitive answers to many of the questions posed by spiritual dilemmas. Curiosity, however, not only benefits a client; it potentially benefits the therapist. A curious therapist may learn something useful to her or his own life.

COMFORT WITH MYSTERY

Spirituality presents more mysteries than definitive conclusions, and so psychotherapists who work with clients regarding their spiritual development are best served by the capacity to tolerate mystery. A therapist who views psychotherapy as a search for an ultimate truth will find work with spirituality frustrating (unless prepared to present the Truth to clients). Psychotherapy can be about truth, but it is a very limited, very personal truth, especially in regard to spirituality.

One aspect of tolerating mystery in psychotherapy is the willingness to see the illumination of questions as being as valuable as the location of answers. Sometimes, the resolution of spiritual dilemmas lies not in arriving at definitive answers but in posing new questions. Indeed, sometimes it is such "definitive" answers that are at the heart of the dilemma. In this way, the psychotherapist is something of a Socratic teacher. However, to be truly effective as a Socratic teacher, the therapist must also respect Socratic irony: that questions posed are genuine and not simply vehicles for bringing a client to a particular viewpoint.

A final metaphor that seems apt to this description of the role that mystery plays in psychotherapy is that, at least in the arena of spiritual development, the journey is much more important than the destination. The therapist is a companion, sometimes a guide, on this journey but is basically as lost on it as the client.

CONTAINMENT, THE CAPACITY
TO TOLERATE CHAOS

With the willingness to be curious and flexible and to tolerate mystery comes an inescapable level of chaos. Therapists do well to tolerate spiritual chaos because it is out of such chaos that a client's most profound truths may come (Myss, 1996).

In the current environment of managed care, with its emphasis on brevity and treatment planning, therapists are not encouraged to learn to tolerate chaos. It is beyond the scope of this book to tilt against the windmill of so-called managed care; however, it is worth noting that psychotherapy focused on understanding spiritual concerns is not so amenable to treatment planning. Therefore, within whatever organizational limitations the therapist works, she or he is well served by the ability to see chaos as a partner rather than an enemy. Although it may be difficult to explain to the insurance company care manager, chaos is the medium of discovery.

The capacity to tolerate chaos has sometimes been labeled containment by the English object relations school. Basically defined, containment refers to the therapist's ability to be with a client without being overwhelmed as that client experiences feelings that threaten to overwhelm her or him. To avoid being overwhelmed, the client sometimes gives such feelings—anxiety, rage, hatred—to the therapist for safekeeping until a time when they can be integrated into the client's identity. This has often been described as the therapist's being able to "sit with" a client's feelings and resultant fantasies until these can be safely reintegrated by that client. In clinical work, the most experience-near term to describe this process is *tolerating chaos*.

Sometimes if we do nothing else for a client, we can aid the person in developing or strengthening his or her own ability to tolerate chaos. This capacity is one of the most important that a person can possess in the modern world. In the arena of spiritual functioning, the capacity to tolerate chaos often aids clients in arriving at conclusions that have previously been too difficult to reach because of the fear of being overwhelmed. Put simply, the capacity to tolerate chaos can be enormously beneficial in allowing a client to move from a spiritual quagmire in which he or she has been struggling, sometimes for many years, and all the while sinking.

EMPATHY

Empathy is perhaps the most widely studied and argued concept in psychotherapy. It is the central concept of at least two major schools of psychotherapy: the person-centered approach and self psychology. Although each defines the term a little differently, there are two key similarities. First, the experience of empathy is crucial to the development of a cohesive, integrated, and congruent identity. Second, the experience of being empathically responded to in psychotherapy can ameliorate difficulties in identity cohesion and congruence (Kahn, 1985, 1989; Rowe & Mac Isaac, 1989).

The use of empathy in psychotherapy has been the source of conceptual disagreements as well. Within the psychoanalytic tradition, empathy has been viewed as the capacity for vicarious introspection, which then informs interpretations to the client. Empathy was thus originally treated as a preliminary step to interpretation. The communication of the vicarious introspection itself was not considered essential or even desirable. Self psychology modified this traditional view a great deal; however, there is still controversy within this model regarding whether interpretation or direct empathic comment is the more helpful mode of responding to the client.

Within the person-centered approach, there is controversy as well. Although Rogers himself (1975, 1980) described empathy as "a way of being," idiosyncratic to each therapist and every psychotherapeutic relationship (even to different moments within the same relationship), many person-centered practitioners have confused empathy with reflective listening. Rogers often maintained that *his* way of being empathic was to listen reflectively; however, this was not *the* way of being empathically responsive (Bozarth, 1984).

The creation of an empathic ambiance seems much more important than what the therapist does verbally. Two other attitudinal qualities are important components of empathic responsiveness: the capacity and willingness to see reality as relative and the related capacity and willingness to suspend disbelief in listening to a client's story.

The relativity of reality seems to be one of the most difficult concepts to communicate to scientifically minded Westerners. Our culture encourages seeing the world as composed of immutable and irrefutable realities. Objects are solid; natural laws are unchangeable. The suggestion that much of "objective reality" is actually dependent on perception and definition is anxiety provoking to many people and often simply dismissed out of hand. This dismissal does not obviate the phenomenon, alluded to in Chapter 1, that one hundred people witnessing the same event will give nearly one hundred varying accounts of what they witnessed. It therefore behooves the psychotherapist to treat "reality" as relative to the persons, usually the client and therapist, involved. Put simply, the capacity to tolerate multiple views of "reality" is extremely important in a psychotherapeutic experience that seeks to aid a client in spiritual development. Even for a therapist who considers herself or himself an expert on other aspects of "objective reality" (e.g., natural phenomena), it is important to approach spiritual phenomena with a humility admitting of multiple potential versions of "reality."

A second component of empathic responsiveness, intimately related to the first, is the ability and willingness to suspend disbelief when listening to a client's story. Literature and cinema both rely heavily on an audience's willingness to suspend disbelief in order to grasp the larger message of the work. The psychotherapist is best served by being this type of audience as well.

Clients present us with a storyline that contains a larger message. Memories of events and feelings are organized around the communication of this larger message. It is important that we understand the larger message and not become bogged down in details that seem doubtful to us. Especially in the area of spiritual functioning, the ability to listen to a client's storyline as a vehicle for a broader message, essentially as we would in watching a play, serves us well. The capacity to suspend disbelief also has the tendency to reduce client resistance organized around the therapist's challenging of the details of memories, perceptions, or feelings.

AMPLIFICATION

Thus far, the conceptualization offered regarding empathic responsiveness concerns its attitudinal nature. There seems to be an operational conceptualization as well—one that concerns what could be labeled *amplification* (Cornett, 1993, 1995). Amplification refers to the process whereby the psychotherapist attempts to capture the nuances of what a client is saying and communicate them back, allowing the client to experience them more fully. At times, amplification is equivalent to Rogers's reflective listening; at other times, it is somewhat different. An example of this difference can be seen in the following conversation between a therapist and client:

Client: "I'm really mad at my wife. Last night she led me to believe that we were going to have sex, but then when we got into bed, she said she was too tired."

Therapist: "You're angry with her because it felt like she teased you. Is that it?" In this brief interchange, the therapist amplifies, by putting into different words, what he understands the client to be saying, perhaps offering the client a new way of conceptualizing what he is feeling and why. This differs from reflective listening in that it moves slightly beyond what the client is saying to present it back to the client in a slightly modified conceptualization. It does not seek to change what the client is saying, thinking, or feeling, only to describe these feelings or thoughts more evocatively.

Amplification can be quite important in spiritually attuned psychotherapy because it draws out feelings or thoughts that the client leaves in the background. It can be especially important for clients who are frightened of what they perceive as negative feelings like hatred or anger. By amplifying the feelings or thoughts that seem to be present, but only in the shadows, the therapist can bring them out into the light where discussion is possible.

THE EXAMINED LIFE

According to Plato, Socrates once asserted that "the unexamined life is not worth living." Whether or not this is true for everyone is debatable. For the psychotherapist, however, it is arguably more true. In looking over the list of attitudinal qualities presented above as characterizing the effective psychotherapist, one could argue that psychotherapists must be born, not made. To a limited extent, this is true. Some individuals seem more amenable by disposition and constitution to be psychotherapists than others. But this is not the final determination. Spiritually attuned psychotherapists can be made, provided that they are willing to examine their own lives.

One of the cornerstones of psychoanalytic training has traditionally been a personal training analysis for the aspiring analyst. Historically, other mental health professions also required or strongly encouraged their students or young practitioners to be involved in some type of therapeutic experience. This commitment of novice and experienced practitioners to learn part of their craft from the experience of being a client is decreasing. As a result, there seem to be an increasing number of young practitioners who are unaware of the personal dynamics they bring to their therapeutic work. Although the managed care environment is built on the notion that technical expertise is the deciding factor in psychotherapy, this never has been the case, and it never will. As Laing points out, psychotherapy is an attempt between two human beings to reclaim the wholeness and complexity of their humanity. It is not the lancing of a boil or the replacement of a transmission. Whereas the surgeon or the mechanic may gain technical expertise without the exploration of his or her own internal world, the psychotherapist will forever be incomplete without such exploration. This is nowhere else truer than in the area of spirituality.

TRANSFERENCE AND THE APPLICATION OF TECHNIQUE

The concept of transference has a long history in psychoanalysis. Freud (1912) identified the focus on transference as one of the defining characteristics of psychoanalysis. Understanding transference phenomena continues to be an important aspect of psychodynamically oriented psychotherapy. It is within the context of responding to a client's transference reactions that the technique outlined above becomes most important.

Traditionally, transference has been understood as the projection of unresolved familial patterns, especially oedipal fantasies and memories, onto the therapist. This projection distorts the relationship

between the therapist and the client. Ostensibly, this distortion parallels distortions present in other relationships. By helping the client
understand these distortions, the therapist helps the client see the dys-
functional patterns that interfere in relationships.

As with so many other clinical issues, the interpersonal school and
self psychology propose important revisions to the traditional theory of
transference. First, both models disagree that transference always represents oedipally based dynamics. Especially in the case of self psychology, transference phenomena are conceptualized as being based on
narcissistic yearnings. Second, both argue against seeing transference
as a distortion of an otherwise "real relationship" between the client
and therapist. Fromm (1980) articulately argues against this conception of transference because it places the psychotherapist in the role of
arbiter of reality and relegates the client to the position of a child who
is ignorant of reality. The interpersonal school also argues that transference is not a distortion in the sense that it defines the therapist as other
than he or she is. Indeed, interpersonalists propose that transference
phenomena are always based on real aspects of the therapist, although
they are generally somewhat exaggerated (Winer, 1994). Thus, if a
client perceives the therapist as overly critical, harsh, punitive, indeci-
sive, or something else, these qualities can be found in some measure in
the therapist.

It is in responding to transference phenomena that the therapist
employs the attitudinal aspects and related activities of technique
described earlier. Though generally less important in psychotherapy
than in psychoanalysis, working through transference manifestations
can still be an important aspect of treatment. In working with spiritual
issues, transference phenomena can take on broader characteristics
than have traditionally been conceived. For instance, transference
reactions can give the therapist clues to the perspective a client takes
toward spiritual issues, including ideas about God. In addition to offering the opportunity for a client to clarify interpersonal patterns and
expectations, working with a client to understand the spiritual ramifications of transference phenomena can increase satisfaction in the
spiritual area of development. James, a twenty-nine-year-old man seen

in weekly psychotherapy, presented opportunities to look at transference manifestations and technique in regard to spiritual issues.

James came to my office initially complaining of difficulty finding satisfying relationships. He also complained of generally feeling empty and anxious. He was employed at a skilled technical job. Although a man of limited formal education, he was extremely bright and articulate. This was one of the first aspects that stood out about James. He clearly was a man who could have done well in any academic or intellectual pursuit: however, he had settled for a job that was somewhat physically demanding but made very little use of his intellectual capacities. I became aware of my sense that he was underutilizing his talents and a vague wish that he would return for more formal education. It was important that I acknowledge this as one of my values and attempt to hold it in abeyance. Perhaps James did not value education in the way that I do. Perhaps he had discovered a path that made more sense for him. Immediately I was left with a question about James and a reminder to myself to monitor the role my own values took in his therapy.

James was from a small family in the Northeast. Both of his parents were employed as professionals and earned comfortable livings. He had a brother and sister, both younger, who lived near their parents. James had moved quite a distance. Initially, I asked why he had moved so far from the rest of the family, and he gave a series of only marginally related sentences that suggested he had followed a number of jobs and simply wound up in this particular locale.

As we began to talk about his family, he was very guarded, and I began to notice that any time his parents were discussed, his typical level of articulate speech would deteriorate. He would begin to stammer and have great difficulty in communicating a sense of what he was attempting to say. During one session I brought this to his attention, and he became noticeably anxious.

He asked me pointedly, "What are you saying?"

Feeling as if I had been somewhat injurious, I attempted to reassure him by saying, "I was just offering the observation that your anxiety seems to increase as you talk about your parents."

As if not even hearing me, he responded somewhat blankly, "I don't think that means I'm stupid."

I was somewhat surprised by this turn in our interaction and said, "Do you think that was what I was saying?"

"No, never mind."

I tried for a few more moments to engage him in looking at what seemed to be a very significant interaction between us, without success.

Our work focused extensively on his developmental years. He had perceived himself, the oldest, as being something of a "guinea pig" for his parents. He felt that they had been harsher with him than his younger siblings. However, he would continuously dismiss this as being unimportant "because they didn't know any better."

At one point, I challenged this and asked, "Well, even if we accept the possibility that they didn't know any better, does that make it any less hurtful?"

"Well, no, but it means that there is really nothing for me to complain about."

This provided us the first opportunity to talk about the possibility that one can have very strong feelings of anger and pain about something that cannot necessarily be changed. He may have been correct that his parents could have done no better, but that did not mean that their behavior toward him was not hurtful. This was not a concept with which he was familiar.

As our work began to move into a more interactive mode, with his offering less historical information and the two of us processing information we had gathered (approximately the sixth month of his therapy), I began to notice another pattern. In addition to his increased anxiety when talking about parents or interactions in the present that might be parentally influenced, he seemed to have some difficulty in comprehending many of my comments to him. I would offer a thought and he would stare blankly at me for a moment and then essentially plead that he did not understand. I was reminded of our early interaction in which he thought I was saying he was stupid. I immediately began to wonder if I was beginning to play a role that involved his perceiving himself in relation to me as being "stupid," and my behaving in a way that somehow played into this (e.g., using words that might be more easily communicated another way). At one point, I commented on this possibility.

"You know," I began, "it seems like there are often times when I say things that are difficult to understand. I wonder what that is about?"

"Probably just that I'm stupid." James remarked with a bland look.

"There's that word again."

"What word?"

"I heard it once early in our work together, when you asked me if I was calling you stupid."

"Uh, I don't remember."

"I'm beginning to wonder if it is possible that we are seeing something very important unfold between us. That is, when you talk about your parents, you become increasingly anxious, and your typical level of understanding, which is highly insightful, begins to be replaced by a type of numbness." James looked interested in what I was saying, and I was attempting to pick my words very carefully to avoid any hint of criticism. "At those moments," I continued, "it seems that you step into a role where you are expecting me to be more intelligent than you and ultimately to criticize you for that. On at least one occasion, you have commented on hearing me do so, when you thought I called you stupid. However, if I don't seem to do that, you will step up to the plate and do it yourself."

He laughed nervously.

"So I guess I'm wondering if we are seeing an important pattern between you and your parents, that is, that you often felt 'stupid' in relationship to them."

At this point, a tear came to James's eye, and he began to talk about his sense that he had always felt "stupid" with them. They had continually criticized him for doing poorly at his school work, even though he made average or above grades. Ultimately, they told him that his school performance did not merit his going to college, and they would not be willing to pay for him to do so.

As he finished, I was struck by the ferocity of his parents' anger toward him and the opportunities that had been closed for him. I made some comment to that effect.

James looked thoughtfully at me for a moment and then asked quite sincerely, "That's the way it's supposed to be, isn't it?"

"Is it?" I asked.

"Well, yeah. After all, some of us are born with native abilities, and some of us aren't. I suppose I wasn't, no crying about that, just kind of the way it is."

"So why do you think you would be born with a lack of this 'native ability'?"

"I don't know, I guess that's just the way it was supposed to be." His look was one of serenity in accepting that there was some cosmic rule suggesting that some people are born limited and must simply play out the hand dealt to them, while others experience much more ease in life.

At this point, I was aware that we were beginning to wander into a spiritual area. I again attempted to open it up for him by asking, "So, what force would impose such a law on the universe?"

"Huh, I don't know. I guess God."

"And why would God impose such a law?"

"Because he needs to be above us all. There need to be levels of things. You see?"

"Not yet."

"God's the smartest being. Then there are levels of beings—I guess angels—that are one step below him. Then there are smart people. Then there are average people. Then there are people who are much less than average."

"Okay. So why was this system set up?"

James looked thoughtful for a moment and did not seem to have a ready answer. However, after a few moments, he said, "Well, I guess so that there would always be people who could lead and those who would follow."

I was struck by the simplicity of his answer and wondered how his conception of God would fit into this view. I verbalized my question aloud.

"Well, God's the smartest of them all. That's why we are supposed to worship him. He set up the universe, and you know how complicated the universe is. He created everything, and it took a lot of intelligence to do that. We should be thankful to him and worship him for how smart he is."

Over the next few months, work with James proceeded along understanding his parents' view of the world, which was that they were intelligent and he was not (even though this was not realistically the case). We began to understand James's conception of the spiritual nature of the universe as being narcissistically organized, that his god had to be more intelligent than everyone else in order to maintain a rightful place in it. James, in a corollary way, had to be much less intelligent than his god to keep his rightful place. The parallels between this god and James's parents were obvious and understandable.

About a year into his therapy, James began to get a more emotional understanding of his spiritual ordering of the universe through our relationship. He had long considered me more intelligent than him, although this was not the case. As a result, he had often deferred to me about important issues, which I would then comment upon. Importantly, the pattern of my sometimes interacting with him in ways that would heighten his sense of my intelligence versus his (using psychological jargon, for example) still occurred on occasion. At these moments I would attempt to become aware of my doing that and on one occasion joked with him, "Whoops, I have become your parents again."

After about a year of therapy, James became increasingly withdrawn. He had always been an active participant in therapy and enthusiastic about appointments. Now, he began to be late for his appointments. On one occasion, he missed an appointment entirely, and when I called to follow up with him, he said distractedly, "Oh, I must have forgotten." In the session following this missed appointment, we explored what seemed to be the developing pattern of his losing interest in therapy. Initially he seemed to be as baffled by his loss of interest as I was. However, there gradually came an edge in his voice that betrayed some anger toward me. As I pointed this out to him, he noted his awareness of it as well. Over the next couple of sessions, the edge turned from something of a glowing ember into a noticeable flame. Still, we attempted to understand the motivations for these feelings. I attributed them initially to a part of his resistance that had also been expressed in his absences and tardiness for appointments.

Finally, after several sessions of this, James made a declaration: "I don't get it, I just don't think this is doing any good."

I sat quietly thinking about the change from being angered to his seeming sadness and disappointment. Suddenly it occurred to me that perhaps we were still talking about his spiritual world, and I asked about this.

"What do you mean?" he asked.

"Well, I'm not sure. It seems like we were talking about the importance of your spirituality and your understanding of your place in the universe, when all of this began. Perhaps there is some connection."

At that moment, something did seem to change with James, and he became alive in the session again. He said, "Well I guess I know what it might be."

I nodded, encouraging him to go on.

"Well, I thought I used to understand what God was about. Now I'm not so sure. I've been thinking a lot about how difficult it is to understand anything else when that part of it is gone."

At that point, his resistance and anger made perfect sense to me. We had begun to challenge his very fundamental beliefs about the operation of the universe and his place in it. He was resisting that change.

Over the next few months, we continued to explore the disappointment and fear he experienced in looking at a new conception of the universe. However, something else began to emerge from this that was new. James began to talk about an identification with me that included a sense of my empathy and acceptance of him. This stood in stark contrast to his parents'—and ultimately his god's—demand that he fit a particular role and that that role be subservient to them. He ultimately began to talk about the possibility that God might be a being of acceptance and understanding rather than narcissistic demands. His level of curiosity increased. With this increase also came an increase in his empathy.

One of James's initial complaints concerned having few meaningful relationships. As his empathy developed more fully, he developed some stable and affirming friendships. He found someone who was of interest romantically.

Therapy with James lasted almost three years. At its conclusion, he related that a great deal had changed in his life for the better. In addition to the positive changes in his relationships, his spirituality had moved in a more affirming direction. His god no longer simply viewed James as "stupid." Like James himself, his god became more curious and empathic.

As is always the case, these changes were the result of a variety of factors. I would argue that a continual focus on the relationship that developed between us was one of the most important.

CONCLUSION

Spiritually attuned psychotherapeutic technique is primarily an attitudinal phenomenon, grounded in therapists' willingness to attempt to understand themselves. This type of technique requires that therapists develop an understanding of their own identities, which allows them to approach their clients with a set of qualities and related activities that increase clients' interest in and acceptance of their humanity. In this acceptance lies the healing of psychotherapy.

AUTHENTIC AND AFFIRMING SPIRITUALITY

FINAL THOUGHTS

Spirituality is an intimate part of human life. Throughout time, people have attempted to understand why things are as they are. More important, they have attempted to understand how they are meant to fit into the order of the universe. Spirituality is the first defining characteristic of the human being, and it should probably be considered one of the most important focuses of psychotherapy. It is more universal than some other developmental phenomena that form the bulwark of psychotherapeutic theory. For instance, there is no anthropological research that confirms the universal nature of the oedipal conflict. There is little doubt that in sexually repressed, middle-class, Victorian Vienna, the oedipal conflict was both clinically observable and a legitimate focus of psychotherapeutic efforts. Whether the oedipal conflict continues to meet both these criteria is debatable. This aside, Freud (1913) himself acknowledged the universal nature of spiritual strivings, even though he described their basic motivations with constructs from his newly created psychoanalysis.

REPRISE

Despite the enormous evidence that spirituality is a quintessential element of the human condition, psychotherapy has generally been loath to see it as a legitimate area for exploration and dialogue with clients, even when many clients are clearly struggling with spiritual conflicts. It is as though psychotherapists become deaf when spirituality is brought up by clients.

Deafness toward the spiritual conflicts of clients' lives is slowly beginning to change. The danger now is that the more traditional and intellectually rigorous schools of psychotherapy are not responding as quickly as those that are part of the new age movement. I would not denigrate the very real assistance that some clients have found here; nevertheless, psychotherapy based primarily on new age principles does not offer the sophistication in understanding human dilemmas that one hundred years of psychotherapeutic experience and research do. Some clinician-theoreticians (Gay, 1989a, 1989b) are applying the hard-won insights of traditional psychodynamic models, especially self psychology, to spirituality. This needs to happen with all clinicians. This is a time of deep frustration and confusion. The pillars that supported both the individual and culture—church, extended family, social roles—are diminishing. Many of us have welcomed the freedom that this loosening of tradition has brought but do not see, or perhaps have ignored, the enormous price such freedom exacts. Ours is an age of freedom, but also of confusion and frustration. Each passing day, this combination seems to foment a host of social problems and adds to an increasing lack of civility, especially in Western culture. I agree with Hillman and Ventura (1992) that we have had a century of psychotherapy and the world is, in many ways, worse in spite of it. One aspect of why this seems to be so is that psychotherapy has focused on a variety of issues during this century but largely ignored humanity's most basic spiritual dilemmas.

Psychotherapy need not be spiritually insensitive. It is best served by conceptualizing spirituality as a developmental phenomenon like any other. Just as other developmental phenomena comprise various and disparate elements, so does spirituality. Some of these components might include the search for meaning in life, values, an understanding of mortality, a conceptualization of how the universe is organized and guided, beliefs regarding the dilemma of suffering, and beliefs regarding the nature of transcendence or the fate of individual identity after death.

Parents play a significant role in the development of a spiritual viewpoint. It is in those first experiences of dependence on another for basic life sustenance that we learn the first lessons that ultimately shape our cosmologies. Perhaps the most important lesson during this developmental experience is whether the universe welcomes us with joy or tolerates us with sufferance. Perhaps the first and most important lesson learned from primary caregivers—one with a profound impact both on later relationships and on the conception of our god—is whether there is enough love to go around.

Love and hatred form the foundation of human emotional life. The most important aspect determining the ability to love others is the capacity to love the self, yet self-love, or narcissism, is discouraged by Western culture. Narcissistic development, until the work of Kohut, was associated with psychopathology. Kohut illuminated the fact that narcissistic development is an inherent part of identity development and that it is only from a stable identity that we are able to share love with others. An individual's spiritual view deeply influences how much love can be allocated to the self. Psychotherapy must understand the intimate relationship between the spiritual worldview of the individual and narcissistic development.

Paradoxically, as Western culture discourages love of the self, it also discourages the experience and expression of hatred. Hatred and love are the twin pillars of emotional development and support all other derivative emotions. It seems reasonable to assert that ours is a culture deeply conflicted about feelings. Traditional forms of religion and spirituality have bolstered that conflict. Yet feelings arise, bidden or not, and must be integrated into our identities. One critical task of the psychotherapist is to aid clients in the integration of both love and hatred into their lives. To do this, the therapist must be prepared to explore the most intimate relational and spiritual aspects of a client's life.

One of the ways that our culture has sought to deal with its conflicts regarding love and hatred has been through encouragement of the natural human tendency to seek security through moral absolutism. Western culture is perhaps more polarized than at any other time in history. People embrace absolute views of "right" and "wrong" on opposing sides of the religious and political spectrums. This is the dilemma in macroview. The psychotherapist often witnesses the embrace of moral absolutism in clients desperately searching for stability and security, yet this embrace has deleterious consequences to a rich and complex emotional life. To the psychotherapist often falls the task of helping clients embrace a wide range of complicated and contradictory feelings. To do so, the therapist must be prepared to look with the client at the spiritual foundations of her or his moral stance.

Psychotherapists must have as much knowledge as possible of the internal dynamics that influence their perceptions and the actions based on those perceptions. Traditionally, this has been the realm of countertransference management. In looking with clients at their spiritual lives, therapists must know as much as possible about the values they hold regarding spirituality. To strive to know our values and prevent them from dominating a client's life is deeply respectful and affirming of that person. A willingness to monitor our own internal worlds also offers the opportunity for us to grow. This is one of the reciprocal gifts of psychotherapy.

Finally, psychotherapists aid their clients by what they do and, more important, by who they are. There are attitudinal qualities that almost obviate the need for specific techniques. This is a notion that goes somewhat against the grain of traditional conceptions of psychotherapeutic technique, yet in an area where so little can be definitively known, it is only common sense. To draw on specific techniques requires that the goal or end point of an endeavor be known. This is a luxury not afforded those psychotherapists willing to search with their clients for spiritual meaning.

FUTURE CHALLENGES

Probably the most significant challenge facing the mental health professions currently is the integration of diverse fields of knowledge. With each passing day, there seems to be new knowledge offered from a variety of disciplines that touches both psychotherapeutic theory and practice. One source of such knowledge is the burgeoning field of genetics. Another is biological psychiatry. Both of these medically based fields are constantly challenging practitioners to rethink their guiding theories and methodologies. Change is difficult for most people; psychotherapists are no exception. This notwithstanding, it is critical that we keep abreast of new theories and data.

The integration of spirituality represents a similar challenge to clinicians, as well as supervisors and institutions that train budding psychotherapists. Yet it offers a different challenge as well. Whereas medically based disciplines can offer hard data—brain scans, PET scans, genetic markers, and so forth—to support their contentions, some areas of human functioning can never be quantified or, sometimes, even observed. There is an elegance to this mystery that demands our acknowledgment and respect. It is therefore incumbent on mental health educators to develop in students the flexibility to embrace that which seems provable "scientifically" but never to be led into believing that all that is important can thus be proved. At a time when psychotherapy is increasingly pressured to give up the respect for mystery in favor of quick, demonstrable results, this mind-set is ever more important.

Those of us who are practitioners and those who would be practitioners live in an exciting time. We have at our disposal, more than ever before, a range of ways to aid clients. Yet perhaps the most important tool is one that is as old as psychotherapy itself: the dogged desire to remain true to the heart of our craft, the human soul.

References

American Psychiatric Association (1994). Diagnostic and statistical manual of mental disorders (4th edition). Washington, DC: APA.

Armstrong, K. (1993). A history of God: The 4000-year quest of Judaism, Christianity, and Islam. New York: Knopf.

Atwood, G. (1989). Psychoanalytic phenomenology and the thinking of Martin Heidegger and Jean-Paul Sartre. In D. Detrick & S. Detrick (Eds.), Self psychology: Comparisons and contrasts (pp. 193–211). Hillsdale, NJ: Analytic Press.

Becker, E. (1973). The denial of death. New York: Free Press.

Bennett, W. (1993). The book of virtues: A treasury of great moral stories. New York: Simon & Schuster.

Bettelheim, B. (1982). Freud and man's soul. New York: Vintage Books.

Boswell, J. (1994). Same-sex unions in premodern Europe. New York: Villard Books.

Bozarth, J. (1984). Beyond reflection: Emergent modes of empathy. In R. Levant & J. Shlien (Eds.), Client-centered therapy and the person-centered approach: New directions in theory, research, and practice (pp. 59–75). New York: Praeger.

Bozarth, J. (1990). The essence of client-centered therapy. In G. Lietaer, J. Rombauts, & R. Van Balen (Eds.), Client-centered and experiential psychotherapy in the nineties (pp. 59–64). Leuven, Belgium: Leuven University Press.

Bromberg, P. (1989). Interpersonal psychoanalysis and self psychology: A clinical comparison. In D. Detrick & S. Detrick (Eds.), Self psychology: Comparisons and contrasts (pp. 275–291). Hillsdale, NJ: Analytic Press.

Bromberg, W. (1975). From shaman to psychotherapist: A history of the treatment of mental illness. Chicago: Henry Regnery Co.

Burr, V. (1995). An introduction to social constructionism. London: Routledge.

Castelnuovo-Tedesco, P. (1991). On "small" physical defects and the sense of being defective. In P. Castelnuovo-Tedesco (Ed.), Dynamic psychiatry: Explorations in psychotherapy, psychoanalysis, and psychosomatic medicine (pp. 225–242). Madison, CT: International Universities Press.

Coles, R. (1970). Erik Erikson: The growth of his work. New York: DaCapo Press.

Coles, R. (1995). The mind's fate. Boston: Little, Brown.

Cornett, C. (1985). The cyclical pattern of child physical abuse from a psychoanalytic self-psychology perspective. *Child and Adolescent Social Work Journal, 2,* 83–92.

Cornett, C. (1992a). Beyond words: A conception of self psychology. *Clinical Social Work Journal, 20,* 337–341.

Cornett, C. (1992b). Toward a more comprehensive personology: Integrating a spiritual perspective into social work practice. *Social Work, 37,* 101–102.

Cornett, C. (1993). Dynamic psychotherapy of gay men: A view from self psychology. In C. Cornett (Ed.), *Affirmative dynamic psychotherapy with gay men* (pp. 45–76). Northvale, NJ: Jason Aronson.

Cornett, C. (1995). *Reclaiming the authentic self: Dynamic psychotherapy with gay men.* Northvale, NJ: Jason Aronson.

Cushman, P. (1992). Psychotherapy to 1992: A historically situated interpretation. In D. Freedheim (Ed.), *History of Psychotherapy: A century of change* (pp. 21–64). Washington, DC: American Psychological Association.

Cushman, P. (1995). *Constructing the self, constructing America: A cultural history of psychotherapy.* Reading, MA: Addison-Wesley.

Diggins, J. (1992). *The rise and fall of the American left.* New York: Norton.

Elkins, D. (1995). Psychotherapy and spirituality: Toward a theory of the soul. *Journal of Humanistic Psychology, 35,* 78–98.

Ellenberger, H. (1970). *The discovery of the unconscious: The history and evolution of dynamic psychiatry.* New York: Basic Books.

Feldmann, T., & Johnson, P. (1995). The application of psychotherapeutic and self psychology principles in hostage negotiations. *Journal of the American Academy of Psychoanalysis, 23,* 207–221.

Fine, R. (1979). *A history of psychoanalysis.* New York: Columbia University Press.

Freud, S. (1912). The dynamics of transference. In J. Strachey (Ed. and Trans.), *The standard edition of the complete psychological works of Sigmund Freud* (Vol. 12, pp. 99–108). London: Hogarth Press, 1958.

Freud, S. (1913). Totem and taboo. In J. Strachey (Ed. and Trans.), *The standard edition of the complete psychological works of Sigmund Freud* (Vol. 13, pp. 1–161). London: Hogarth Press, 1955.

Freud, S. (1923). The ego and the id. In J. Strachey (Ed. and Trans.), *The standard edition of the complete psychological works of Sigmund Freud* (Vol. 19, pp. 12–59). London: Hogarth Press, 1961.

Freud, S. (1924). The dissolution of the Oedipus complex. In J. Strachey (Ed.

and Trans.), *The standard edition of the complete psychological works of Sigmund Freud* (Vol. 19, pp. 173–179). London: Hogarth Press, 1961.

Freud, S. (1927). The future of an illusion. In J. Strachey (Ed. and Trans.), *The standard edition of the complete psychological works of Sigmund Freud* (Vol. 21, pp. 5–58). London: Hogarth Press, 1961.

Freud, S. (1939). Moses and monotheism. In J. Strachey (Ed. and Trans.), *The standard edition of the complete psychological works of Sigmund Freud* (Vol. 23, pp. 7–137). London: Hogarth Press, 1964.

Fromm, E. (1950). *Psychoanalysis and religion*. New Haven: Yale University Press.

Fromm, E. (1980). *Greatness and limitations of Freud's thought*. New York: Mentor.

Galatzer-Levy, R., & Cohler, B. (1993). *The essential other: A developmental psychology of the self*. New York: Basic Books.

Gay, P. (1988). *Freud: A life for our time*. New York: Norton.

Gay, V. (1989a). Philosophy, psychoanalysis and the problem of change. *Psychoanalytic Inquiry, 9*, 26–44.

Gay, V. (1989b). *Understanding the occult: Fragmentation and repair of the self*. Minneapolis: Fortress Press.

Gilligan, C. (1983). *In a different voice*. Cambridge: Harvard University Press.

Goldberg, J. (1993). *The dark side of love: The positive role of our negative feelings—anger, jealousy, and hate*. New York: Tarcher/Putnam.

Grosskurth, P. (1986). *Melanie Klein: Her world and her work*. Cambridge: Harvard University Press.

Hanh, T. (Speaker). (1991). *The art of mindful living: How to bring love, compassion, and inner peace into your daily life* (Cassette Recording). Boulder, CO: Sounds True Audio.

Hartmann, H. (1960). *Psychoanalysis and moral values*. New York: International Universities Press.

Hillman, J. (1996). *The soul's code: In search of character and calling*. New York: Random House.

Hillman, J., & Ventura, M. (1992). *We've had a hundred years of psychotherapy and the world's getting worse*. San Francisco: HarperCollins.

Hoffman, M. (1979). Development of moral thought, feeling, and behavior. *American Psychologist, 34*, 958–966.

Hogan, R. (1973). Moral conduct and character: A psychological perspective. *Psychological Bulletin, 79*, 217–232.

Hunter, J. (1994). *Before the shooting begins: Searching for democracy in America's culture wars*. New York: Free Press.

Isay, R. (1993). On the analytic therapy of homosexual men. In C. Cornett (Ed.), *Affirmative dynamic psychotherapy with gay men* (pp. 23–44). Northvale, NJ: Jason Aronson.

James, W. (1902). *The varieties of religious experience*. London: Longmans, Green.

Jamison, K. (1995). *An unquiet mind: A memoir of moods and madness*. New York: Random House.

Josephs, L. (1995). *Balancing empathy and interpretation: Relational character analysis*. Northvale, NJ: Jason Aronson.

Jung, C. (1963). *Memories, dreams, reflections* (R. Winston & C. Winston, Trans.). New York: Pantheon Books.

Kahn, E. (1985). Heinz Kohut and Carl Rogers: A timely comparison. *American Psychologist, 40,* 893–904.

Kahn, E. (1989). Carl Rogers and Heinz Kohut: On the importance of valuing the self. In D. Detrick & S. Detrick (Eds.), *Self psychology: Comparisons and contrasts* (pp. 213–228). Hillsdale, NJ: Analytic Press.

Kawai, H. (1996). *Buddhism and the art of psychotherapy*. College Station: Texas A&M University Press.

Kernberg, O. (1976). *Object-relations theory and clinical psychoanalysis*. New York: Jason Aronson.

Kirschenbaum, H. (1979). *On becoming Carl Rogers*. New York: Dell.

Kohlberg, L. (1984). *The psychology of moral development*. San Francisco: Harper & Row.

Kohut, H. (1971). *The analysis of the self*. New York: International Universities Press.

Kohut, H. (1977). *The restoration of the self*. New York: International Universities Press.

Kohut, H. (1984). *How does analysis cure?* (Eds. A. Goldberg & P. Stepansky). Chicago: University of Chicago Press.

Kohut, H., & Wolf, E. (1978). The disorders of the self and their treatment: An outline. *International Journal of Psychoanalysis, 59,* 413–425.

Kopp, S. (1972). *If you meet the Buddha on the road kill him! The pilgrimage of psychotherapy patients*. New York: Bantam Books.

Kushner, H. (1981). *When bad things happen to good people*. New York: Random House.

Kushner, H. (1996). *How good do we have to be? A new understanding of guilt and forgiveness*. New York: Random House.

Laing, R. (1967). *The politics of experience*. New York: Pantheon Books.

Laing, R. (1969). *The politics of the family and other essays*. New York: Pantheon Books.

Laing, R. (1970). *Knots*. New York: Pantheon Books.

Laing, R. (Speaker). (1995). *Eros, love and lies* (Cassette Recording). New York: Mystic Fire Audio.

Lasch, C. (1979). *The culture of narcissism: American life in an age of diminishing expectations*. New York: Norton.

Lerner, H. (1985). *The dance of anger*. New York: Harper & Row.

Lerner, M. (1996). *The politics of meaning: Restoring hope and possibility in an age of cynicism*. Reading, MA: Addison-Wesley.

Letourneau, C. (1981). Empathy and stress: How they affect parental aggression. *Social Work, 26*, 383–389.

Levenson, E. (1995). *The fallacy of understanding: An inquiry into the changing structure of psychoanalysis*. Northvale, NJ: Jason Aronson.

Lukoff, D., Lu, F., & Turner, R. (1995). Cultural considerations in the assessment and treatment of religious and spiritual problems. *Psychiatric Clinics of North America, 18*, 467–485.

Mahler, M., Pine, F., & Bergman, A. (1975). *The psychological birth of the human infant*. New York: Basic Books.

Masson, J. (1990). *Final analysis: The making and unmaking of a psychoanalyst*. Reading, MA: Addison-Wesley.

May, H. (1976). *The enlightenment in America*. New York: Oxford University Press.

May, R. (1953). *Man's search for himself*. New York: Norton.

McNamara, R. (1995). *In retrospect: The tragedy and lessons of Vietnam*. New York: Random House.

Menaker, E. (1989). Otto Rank and self psychology. In D. Detrick & S. Detrick (Eds.), *Self psychology: comparisons and contrasts* (pp. 75–87). Hillsdale, NJ: Analytic Press.

Menninger, K. (1973). *Whatever became of sin?* New York: Hawthorn Books.

Miller, A. (1981). *The drama of the gifted child: The search for the true self* (R. Ward, Trans.). New York: Basic Books.

Moore, T. (1992). *Care of the soul: A guide for cultivating depth and sacredness in everyday life*. New York: HarperCollins.

Myss, C. (Speaker). (1996). *Spiritual madness* (Cassette Recording). Boulder, CO: Sounds True Audio.

Orwell, G. (1949/1977). *1984*. San Diego: Harcourt Brace Jovanovich.

Poe, E. (1827/1938). *The complete tales and poems of Edgar Allen Poe*. New York: Random House.

Rank, O. (1964). *Will therapy*. New York: Norton.

Richardson, H. (1990). The problem of liberalism and the good. In R. Douglass, G. Mara, & H. Richardson (Eds.), *Liberalism and the good* (pp. 1–28). New York: Routledge.

Robinson, E. (1991). *The devil discovered: Salem witchcraft 1692*. New York: Hippocrene Books.

Rogers, C. (1942). *Counseling and psychotherapy*. Boston: Houghton Mifflin.

Rogers, C. (1951). *Client-centered therapy*. Boston: Houghton Mifflin.

Rogers, C. (1957). The necessary and sufficient conditions of therapeutic personality change. *Journal of Consulting Psychology, 21*, 95–103.

Rogers, C. (1975). Empathic: An unappreciated way of being. *Counseling Psychologist, 5*, 2–10.

Rogers, C. (1980). *A way of being*. Boston: Houghton Mifflin.

Rowe, C., & Mac Isaac, D. (1989). *Empathic attunement: The "technique" of psychoanalytic self psychology*. Northvale, NJ: Jason Aronson.

Sagan, C. (1996). *The demon-haunted world: Science as a candle in the dark*. New York: Random House.

Sartre, J. (1956). *Being and nothingness*. New York: Gramercy Books.

Schachter-Shalomi, Z. (1991). *Spiritual intimacy: A study of counseling in Hasidism*. Northvale, NJ: Jason Aronson.

Schafer, R. (1983). *The analytic attitude*. New York: Basic Books.

Schmitz, K. (1990). Is liberalism good enough? In R. Douglass, G. Mara, & H. Richardson (Eds.), *Liberalism and the good* (pp. 86–104). New York: Routledge.

Searles, H. (1990). The patient as therapist to his analyst. In R. Langs (Ed.), *Classics in psychoanalytic technique* (rev. ed.) (pp. 103–135). Northvale, NJ: Jason Aronson.

Silverstein, C. (1993). The borderline personality disorder in gay people. In C. Cornett (Ed.), *Affirmative dynamic psychotherapy with gay men* (pp. 240–252). Northvale, NJ: Jason Aronson.

Spiegelman, J., & Miyuki, M. (1985). *Buddhism and Jungian psychology*. Phoenix: Falcon Press.

Spitz, R. (1965). *The first year of life*. New York: International Universities Press.

Stanford, P. (1996). *The devil: A biography*. New York: Henry Holt & Co.

Stern, D. (1985). *The interpersonal world of the infant*. New York: Basic Books.

Sullivan, H. (1953a). *Conceptions of modern psychiatry*. New York: Norton.

Sullivan, H. (1953b). *The interpersonal theory of psychiatry*. New York: Norton.

Sullivan, H. (1954). *The psychiatric interview*. New York: Norton.

Sullivan, H. (1965). *Personal psychopathology*. New York: Norton.

Szasz, T. (1961). *The myth of mental illness*. New York: Harper.

Szasz, T. (1994). Mental illness is still a myth. *Society, 31*, 34–39.

Thompson, M. (1994). *The truth about Freud's technique: The encounter with the real*. New York: New York University Press.

Watson, N. (1984). The empirical status of Rogers's hypotheses of the necessary and sufficient conditions for effective psychotherapy. In R. Levant & J. Shlien (Eds.), *Client-centered therapy and the person-centered approach: New directions in theory, research, and practice* (pp. 17–40). New York: Praeger.

Winer, R. (1994). *Close encounters: A relational view of the therapeutic process*. Northvale, NJ: Jason Aronson.

Wolf, E. (1988). *Treating the self: Elements of clinical self psychology*. New York: Guilford.

Yalom, I. (1980). *Existential Psychotherapy*. New York: Basic Books.

Zimring, F., & Raskin, N. (1992). Carl Rogers and client/person-centered therapy. In D. Freedheim (Ed.), *History of psychotherapy: A century of change* (pp. 629–656). Washington, DC: American Psychological Association.

Index